HABERMAS
AND THE MEDIA

Theory and the Media

John Armitage, *Virilio and the Media*
David Gunkel and Paul Taylor, *Heidegger and the Media*
Philip Howard, *Castells and the Media*
Jaeho Kang, *Walter Benjamin and the Media*
Paul A. Taylor, *Žižek and the Media*
Hartmut Wessler, *Habermas and the Media*
Geoffrey Winthrop-Young, *Kittler and the Media*

HABERMAS AND THE MEDIA

HARTMUT WESSLER

polity

First published in 2018 by Polity Press

Polity Press
65 Bridge Street
Cambridge CB2 1UR, UK

Polity Press
101 Station Landing
Suite 300
Medford, MA 02155, USA

ISBN-13: 978-0-7456-5133-0
ISBN-13: 978-0-7456-5134-7 (pb)

A catalogue record for this book is available from the British Library.
Library of Congress Cataloging-in-Publication Data

Names: Wessler, Hartmut, 1965- author.
Title: Habermas and the media / Hartmut Wessler.
Description: Medford, MA : Polity, 2018. | Includes bibliographical
references and index.
Identifiers: LCCN 2018004839 (print) | LCCN 2018031072 (ebook) | ISBN
9781509530922 (Epub) | ISBN 9780745651330 (hardback) | ISBN 9780745651347
(pbk.)
Subjects: LCSH: Habermas, J?urgen. | Mass media. | Communication.
Classification: LCC B3258.H324 (ebook) | LCC B3258.H324 W47 2018 (print) |
DDC 302.23092--dc23
LC record available at https://lccn.loc.gov/2018004839

Typeset in 10.75 on 14pt Janson Text LT Std by
Servis Filmsetting Ltd, Stockport, Cheshire
Printed and bound in the United Kingdom by Clays Ltd, Elcograph S.p.A.

CONTENTS

ACKNOWLEDGMENTS

My first encounter with Habermas's work dates back to the spring of 1985, my second semester at university. In an introductory theory class I was assigned, together with a group of fellow students, to give a presentation on the "Structural Transformation of the Public Sphere." Back then it was not uncommon for communication studies programs in Germany to have students read Habermas in the original very early on. Later I learned from colleagues in Scandinavia that the same was true in some places there, too. Such early familiarity has its strengths and I am grateful for it. But of course, as young undergraduates we also missed a lot of the wider theoretical ramifications – aspects I only discovered when re-examining familiar pieces and reading more recent ones for the first time in preparation for this book.

The most striking discovery, however, in writing this book for an English-language audience was a difference in discursive context. I realized that the productivity of Habermas's work for media and communication studies is less obvious outside the narrow remit of my home country and must therefore be explained more clearly. Connections to other research in the field must be drawn more explicitly than would have seemed necessary at home. On the other hand it also became clear over the years that scholarly work on deliberation and deliberative democracy, which builds on Habermas in one way or the other, has developed at least as strongly and productively in the US (and other countries) as in Germany and has taken distinct routes that I needed to understand in order to grasp Habermas's international impact.

Writing for an Anglophone audience has thus forced me to take an outside view of my subject and to question parts of what I took for granted. It turned out to be a peculiar kind of intercultural communication. It helped clarify my thinking and made me more critical on average of Habermas's contribution to the field of media and communication studies. It helped me identify areas in which Habermas's work on the media was in need of extension and revision and prompted me to highlight possibilities for further theoretical and empirical elaboration.

For this journey from Habermas through his reception in the English-speaking world and back to his work and its possible extensions, I feel indebted to colleagues and students on both sides of the Atlantic and beyond. On the European side I profited greatly from longer and shorter exchanges with André Bächtiger, Michael Brüggemann, Christiane Eilders, Bernward Gesang, Jostein Gripsrud, Katharina Holzinger, Otfried Jarren, Hallvard Moe, Barbara Pfetsch, Mike Schäfer, Rüdiger Schmitt-Beck, Tanjev Schultz, Jürg Steiner, and Yannis Theocharis. I am particularly indebted to my late colleague Bernhard Peters (1949–2005) for unique first-hand perspectives on Habermas. Outside of Europe I am grateful for long-standing collaborations or brief exchanges with Scott Althaus, Rodney Benson, Rose Maia, Patricia Moy,

John Parkinson, and Matthew Powers. I would also like to acknowledge the Fulbright travel grant that enabled me to spend the spring of 2011 as a visiting scholar at New York University, generously hosted by Rodney Benson.

Closer to home, I am intensely grateful to the current and former members of my research team at the University of Mannheim: Manuel Adolphsen, Chung-hong Chan, Rainer Freudenthaler, Eric Hendriks, Lutz Hofer, Kristina John, Charlotte Löb, Julia Lück, Christoph Niemann-Mall, Eike Rinke, Maria Röder, David Schieferdecker, and Antal Wozniak. In relation to this volume's topic a special thank you goes to Eike Rinke for our long-standing joint work on matters of mediated deliberation, and to Charlotte Löb and Rainer Freudenthaler for our ongoing collaboration in researching mediated public spheres. Patrik Haffner and Jonas Voljanek have helped in stemming the tide of the theoretical and empirical literature. I am especially grateful to Marianne Valigura for her unwavering office support over the years. My colleagues at the Institute for Media and Communication Studies in Mannheim deserve thanks for providing such a stimulating work environment. I have also profited greatly from discussions with students in classes at the University of Mannheim, the University of Zürich, and the Federal University of Minas Gerais, Belo Horizonte (Brazil).

The foundations for my intellectual engagements were laid by my parents, Rudolf Wessler (1927–2007) and Martha-Elisabeth Wessler, and I am more than grateful for their guidance and stimulation. Last but not least, my wife, Marita Hartnack, knows better than anybody that academic work can be a real strain before it becomes a source of satisfaction and happiness. She deserves praise for enduring, encouraging, inspiring, challenging, criticizing, and supporting me beyond any expectation. I wholeheartedly dedicate this book to her.

FIGURES AND TABLES

FIGURES

TABLES

INTRODUCTION

Jürgen Habermas is one of the most important contemporary philosophers and social theorists. His work is widely cited in international academic publications and has deeply influenced media and communication scholars around the world. His unique contribution to theorizing the media revolves around three core concepts, which are closely associated with his name: the public sphere, communicative action, and deliberative democracy. It is no exaggeration to say

- that Habermas discovered the *public sphere* as a distinct sphere of social life in modern societies (Fraser 2009),
- that he developed a distinctive idea of *communicative action* by synthesizing vast areas of extant research in linguistics and sociology, and
- that he is the founding father of the *deliberative tradition* in democratic theory.

All three concepts will be explained in detail later in this book. At this point it is important to note that all three are intimately bound up with "the media." Media are central to the functioning of public spheres. People use media for engaging in, and circulating the outcomes of, communicative action (as well as its opposite, strategic action). And deliberative democracy in large-scale societies is not conceivable without the widespread circulation of ideas and arguments through the media. When Habermas talks about "media" or "the media" he is mostly concerned with mass media like newspapers and television; he has written only scantily about the Internet. But this does not diminish his contribution to communication and media studies even today precisely because his view of the media is so strongly infused with these other three central concepts: Public spheres, communicative action, and deliberation are not bound to *mass* media. On the contrary, today's digital network media can under certain conditions help build public spheres, can enable communicative action, and are vital for a burgeoning deliberative democracy. Habermas's work has retained its stimulating force for contemporary media and communication research precisely because he theorizes not primarily specific types of media, but the quality of societal communication more generally.

BIOGRAPHICAL ROOTS

Before we turn to briefly summarizing Habermas's unique theoretical contributions in the next part of this introduction, a few biographical notes seem important (for a comprehensive biography, see Müller-Doohm 2016). Jürgen Habermas was born on June 18, 1929 in Düsseldorf, Germany, and grew up in the small town of Gummersbach. He was three years old when the Nazis came to power in Germany and fifteen when World War II and the Nazi dictatorship ended. During the last throes of the war Habermas, like most young men born in 1928 and 1929, was ordered to serve as a military helper on the Western front, but fortunately, he was spared from actual armed combat. The experience of dictatorship and war made Jürgen Habermas most susceptible to the promise of freedom and democracy as it developed at least in the Western part of postwar Germany. Habermas finished high school in 1949, the year in which the Federal Republic of Germany was founded. During his university studies in Göttingen, Zürich, and Bonn in the early 1950s he became more and more politicized and critical of the restorative tendencies that marked the tenure of Western Germany's conservative first chancellor Konrad Adenauer. Reflecting on this historical period retrospectively, Habermas wrote in his acceptance speech for the Kyoto Prize (which is seen as something like the Nobel Prize for the humanities): "The continuity of social elites and cultural prejudices through which Konrad Adenauer marshaled consent for his policies was stifling. There had been no break with the past, no new beginning in terms of personnel, no change in mentality – neither a moral renewal nor a revolution of political mindset" (Habermas 2008, 19). It was in this climate that Habermas, at the age of twenty-four, and one year before he finished his doctorate in philosophy, wrote his first public intervention, which appeared in the quality daily *Frankfurter Allgemeine Zeitung*. In this piece, entitled "Thinking with Heidegger against Heidegger," Habermas directly attacked Martin Heidegger, then one of Germany's most prominent philosophers, for the unchanged publication of his 1935 lectures in which he had praised the Nazi movement for its "inner truth and greatness." Habermas's article stirred quite some debate in postwar Germany and established his reputation as an astute critic and strident combatant in public debates.

But there is another personal experience that has prompted Habermas's life-long preoccupation with the possibilities of developing public voice and the benefits of discursive exchange with others. By birth Habermas has a cleft upper lip, and he had to undergo surgery at a very early age. The resulting life-long speech impediment as well as the rejection by his schoolmates deeply sensitized Habermas to how valuable – and endangered – the ability to express oneself publicly can be. "I remember the difficulties I encountered when I tried to make myself understood in class or during break while speaking with my nasal articulation and distorted pronunciation of which I was completely unaware. I had left the haven of family life and its familiar surroundings and had to find my feet in an 'anonymous' domain" (Habermas 2008, 15). The schoolyard is a public space much like the more abstract space of the political public sphere. And both are relatively uncomfortable spaces, which demand audacity in expressing yourself and which carry the risk of rejection. Both in the schoolyard and in the political public sphere we are, Habermas says, entangled with others "in an ever denser and more fragile network of relationships of reciprocal recognition" (Habermas 2008, 17). We run the risk that "reciprocity will be *denied*. The morality of equal respect for everyone is designed to absorb such risks. For it is designed to abolish discrimination and to facilitate the inclusion of the marginalized in the network of reciprocal recognition" (Habermas 2008, 17).

After a brief interlude as a freelance journalist Habermas, in 1956, became the research assistant of Theodor W. Adorno, who had returned from exile and reopened, with Max Horkheimer, the Institute for Social Research in Frankfurt. Since its founding in 1924 the Institute had been the breeding ground of Critical Theory, a multidisciplinary endeavor to critically analyze the modern capitalist societies of the time. Adorno and Horkheimer as well as, among others, Herbert Marcuse, Walter Benjamin, Erich Fromm, and Leo Löwenthal are referred to as the first generation of the Frankfurt School. Habermas would later become the leading protagonist of its second generation. But before this could happen Habermas had to leave the Institute in Frankfurt in 1959, due to Horkheimer's clandestine initiative: Horkheimer found Habermas to be "too political" and refused to accept the latter's postdoctoral thesis, which would have earned him the *venia legendi*, the right to teach at the university in his own right. Habermas instead submitted his postdoctoral thesis at the University of Marburg under the guidance of Wolfgang Abendroth, one of the few openly Marxist philosophers in Germany at the time. This thesis was entitled "The structural transformation of the public sphere" and firmly established Habermas's reputation as a leading social theorist. It also marks the starting point for his life-long preoccupation with the emancipatory potential of rational public debate.

Upon completion of the thesis in 1961 Habermas immediately became professor of philosophy at the University of Heidelberg, and three years later, ironically, moved back to Frankfurt to become Horkheimer's successor. He held the chair of philosophy and sociology at the University of Frankfurt from 1964 to 1971. During the following decade, from 1971 to 1981, Habermas served, with Carl Friedrich von Weizsäcker, as the co-director of the Max Planck Institute for the Study of the Scientific-Technical World in Starnberg, near Munich. This institute quickly became a hotbed of intellectual debate in Germany and beyond, and the breeding ground for many influential ideas circulating both in academia and in public debate. In Starnberg Habermas wrote his magnum opus, *The theory of communicative action*.

In 1983 Habermas returned again to Frankfurt, where he worked as a professor of philosophy until his retirement in 1994. By this time his book *Between facts and norms* had come out. After *The structural transformation of the public sphere* in the 1960s and *The theory of communicative action* in the 1970s and 1980s, *Between facts and norms* marks the third phase of Habermas's thinking, spanning the 1990s and 2000s. In this volume he lays the foundations for a new brand of normative democratic theory, the theory of deliberative democracy. Habermas reconstructs democratic governance as a process of collective opinion-formation and decision-making that is supposed to ensure a more rational process of policy-making. Since his retirement in 1994 Habermas has remained very active and has published almost a dozen books and many more articles both as a scholar and as a public intellectual. He has also received numerous prestigious national and international prizes and awards.

IN A NUTSHELL: HABERMAS'S CONTRIBUTION TO THE STUDY OF THE MEDIA

Habermas first presented his idea of the *public sphere* in his postdoctoral thesis, entitled in full "The structural transformation of the public sphere: An inquiry into a category of bourgeois society." It was published as a book in German as early as 1962, but only translated into English in 1989. This late translation sparked an intense discussion internationally, which is partly documented in *Habermas and the public sphere* (Calhoun 1992). The term "public sphere" is widely used throughout the social sciences and humanities as well as in some strands of public and media debate. Habermas uses the term in a relatively specific fashion and with a normative overtone: The public sphere is a discursive arena in which citizens discuss matters of common concern in such a way that the power of the better argument reigns instead of the socioeconomic position of the speaker. This understanding is normative becomes it carries an element of prescription: Communication in the public sphere *should* engender genuine discussion and help the better argument win. If defined in this way not everything that is on public display or "in the media" contributes to maintaining the public sphere – think about gossip or rumors or "fake news." But newspaper editorials, civil forms of television and radio talk shows as well as some kinds of online discussions do. Habermas's specific normative notion of the public sphere has been criticized, and he responded to this criticism in his "Further reflections on the public sphere" (Habermas 1992), in which he offered a number of important revisions to his early book (see chapter 1 for details). Apart from such explicit critique, the term "public sphere" has also been used rather loosely in many places and has become almost a catch-all term for anything that other people can see or hear. Whenever the term surfaces in writing it is worth ascertaining whether the original Habermasian usage is intended or not in order to avoid confusion.

The second core concept, *communicative action*, was developed in Habermas's magnum opus, *The theory of communicative action*. This two-volume work was first published in German in 1981; the English translation appeared in 1984 (volume 1) and 1987 (volume 2). In its pages Habermas laid a new foundation for his thinking about the role of communication in modern society. The two volumes had been available for some time before Habermas's earlier book *Structural transformation of the public sphere* finally appeared in English in 1989. Not many Anglophone readers of *Structural transformation* had read the *Theory of communicative action*. Therefore the implications of Habermas's new notion of communicative action for understanding

communication in the public sphere was not fully appreci-
ated in academic discussions in the early 1990s. According
to Habermas, communicative action is "action oriented to
reaching understanding" and must be sharply distinguished
from strategic action, that is, "action oriented to success"
(Habermas 1984, 285). When we act in order to create
understanding with our conversational partners we not only
make ourselves understood in linguistic terms; we also aim
at eliciting "rationally motivated voluntary agreement" to
what we say. We consciously or unconsciously want others to
accept that (a) what we say is true; our utterance (b) is in line
with generally acceptable social norms, that is, norms that
in principle everybody involved could agree to; and (c) our
words reflect what we really think. Thus, when we engage
in communicative action, Habermas contends, we involun-
tarily make three validity claims: We claim objective truth,
moral rightness, and subjective truthfulness for what we
have to say. While the *Theory of communicative action* shows
how this complex notion of communication is fundamental
to understanding human activity, the book does not offer in
itself a good theory of the media. In particular, it does not
sufficiently spell out what the role of communicative action
could be in public arenas that transcend face-to-face settings, such as political speech, civic protest, journalism, or
public relations.

It took another major book for Habermas to explicitly
connect his theory of the public sphere with his theory of
communicative action and offer an up-to-date account of the
role of the media in democratic life. In *Between facts and norms*
(German 1992, English 1996) he develops a conception of
democracy that revolves around the notion of *deliberation*.
Deliberation is a form of communication in which various
actors exchange arguments, i.e. opinions and reasons, in
order to arrive at a common solution. The institutions of

liberal democracy – parliaments, governments, independent courts – as well as the actors of civil society – citizens, voluntary associations, social movements, and the media – are described as indispensable sites and drivers of democratic communication. From a deliberative perspective, democracy appears as a large-scale experiment in collective learning rather than just the negotiation of conflicting interests. In mediated public communication the exchange of ideas is performed in front of an audience, be it the big audience of the evening newscast or the small audience of a specialized online discussion forum, or anything in between. In chapter 8 of *Between facts and norms*, entitled "On civil society and the political public sphere," Habermas shows under what conditions public deliberation by citizens and their associations can acquire "communicative power" vis-à-vis state institutions and other power-holders. Habermas's idea of deliberative democracy thus rests on spontaneous bottom-up communication that puts the center of the political system "under siege" without aiming at conquering it (Habermas 1992, 452; 1996, 443).

According to Habermas (1996, 378), the media have a mandate to support the willingness to learn and the capacity to criticize on the part of an "enlightened public," that is, an active, deliberating citizenry. This normative idea about the media's role in democracy is further explicated in Habermas's as yet latest account on the topic, the essay "Political communication in media society: Does democracy still have an epistemic dimension?" (Habermas 2009b). Here the media are situated at the center of a system designed to produce well-considered public opinions through a complex web of input and output flows between political actors, mass media, civil society, and state institutions (Habermas 2009b, 166). And following this idea Habermas remains highly critical of media tycoons such as Rupert Murdoch and Silvio

Berlusconi, but also skeptical of the capacity of online media to contribute meaningfully to deliberative democracy.

OUTLINE OF THIS BOOK

Habermas sets out to tackle some of the most fundamental problems of social theory. His works aim at understanding the nature of human agency and the capacity of societies to learn, and in doing so they strive to integrate a lot of prior research from other authors. Fortunately, Habermas is also a public intellectual who contributes regularly to public debates in Germany and beyond, so that he is well aware of the difficulties posed by academic jargon. Therefore, his texts are sometimes spiced with metaphors that illuminate complex matters. One example is the idea already mentioned that civil society puts the political system "under siege." Another is the idea of "sluices" through which citizens' concerns must be channeled in order to be heard in the centers of political power. Or consider the "osmosis" by which arguments from one arena of public debate permeate into adjacent arenas so as to create a common, border-spanning discussion that transcends the parochial horizons of ever-recurring, familiar positions. Wherever possible, I will use such welcome figurative entry points in this book to explain Habermas's ideas and the debates around them.

The first three chapters of this book trace the development of Habermas's media-related thinking over the past fifty-five years. Chapter 1 starts with the *Structural transformation of the public sphere*, discusses its critics and describes the revisions Habermas offered in 1992. In chapter 2 the notion of communicative action is explained, discussed in relation to the media and contextualized in the overall architecture of Habermas's *Theory of communicative action*. Chapter 3 identifies the role Habermas foresees for the media in a deliberative democracy as presented in *Between facts and norms* and "Political communication in media society."

Chapters 4 to 7 then proceed to offer alternatives to, extensions of, and debates surrounding Habermas's thinking. In chapter 4 I sketch three normative rivals of Habermas's model of deliberative democracy, namely the liberal, the republican, and the agonistic models of democracy, as well as Habermas's response to each. Chapter 5 systematizes the research that has used the concept of deliberativeness to empirically assess the quality of news and discussion media. I focus on quality newspapers, television news, Twitter, and political blogs, and show which of these forums offers the strongest potential for deliberative exchanges of ideas. The result is surprising.

Chapter 6 goes one step further and scrutinizes non-deliberative media content such as satire, mediated protest, and public rituals. I search for the contributions that these forms of public communication can make to genuine societal discussion and learning, even though they are not deliberative themselves. In chapter 7, finally, I consider conceptual debates about how counterpublics and mediated activism should be conceived and offer a nascent perspective on the role of emotions in mediated deliberation.

The concluding chapter aims at pointing to fruitful routes for future media and communication scholarship inspired by Habermas's thinking. His distinctive contribution to the field lies in insisting that mediated communication must remain bound to the project of societal self-emancipation and self-regulation – even in times of increasing commercialization, growing political apathy, and populism. How this bond can be renewed is one of the most exciting and pressing issues for contemporary media and communication research.

One final disclaimer may be in order before we embark on the journey. My aim in this book is to provide something like a Habermas-inspired companion for scholars and students of media and communication. In the later chapters of this book I will highlight what I perceive to be the most pressing and promising issues: securing a reasonable level of deliberative quality in the news and discussions we expose ourselves to; ensuring that non-deliberative media content not only is enjoyable, but contributes new ideas and perspectives to meaningful public debate; and reconciling authentic mediated expression of experience and grievance with a productive mutual engagement that signals respect and helps to substantively address those grievances. In short, I look through the "media lens" when I recount and work with Habermas's theoretical oeuvre. This means that I will not necessarily cover those topics at length that Habermas has written about most recently: the future of European and global governance or the role of religion in public life, for example (for an overview see Jacobson 2017). This is partly due to the fact that I study both transnational public spheres and media debates on religion and secularism in separate projects and publications (see Wessler et al. 2008; Brüggemann and Wessler 2014; Wessler, Rinke, and Löb 2016). But the main reason is of course that this book is not called "Habermas today," but "Habermas and the media." So, here we go.

1

THE BOURGEOIS PUBLIC SPHERE
AND ITS CRITICS

It is no exaggeration to say that Habermas "discovered" the public sphere as a separate social domain – a discovery that "occupies the same rank as a discovery in the natural sciences," as Fraser (2009, 148) writes. The term "public sphere" denotes a "central institution of modern society for which no English word existed before" (p. 148). Briefly put, in Habermas's understanding, the public sphere is an arena in which citizens discuss matters of common concern. This arena emerges as a separate social sphere during the transition of European societies from feudalism, in which the aristocratic class dominated society, to capitalism, which is dominated by the owners of the means of economic production. In the course of this transition the public sphere inserts itself as a third space situated between the sphere of public authority (the state, as we would call it today) on the one side and the private sphere of economic reproduction and family life on the other. Figure 1.1 illustrates this insertion of the public sphere

Private realm		Sphere of public authority
Private sphere	*Public sphere*	
Civil society (realm of commodity exchange and social labor)	*Public sphere* in the political realm *Public sphere* in the world of letters (clubs, press)	State (realm of the "police")
Conjugal family's internal space (bourgeois intellectuals)	"Town" (market of cultural products)	Court (courtly-noble society)

Figure 1.1 Blueprint of the bourgeois public sphere in the eighteenth century (adapted from Habermas 1989a, 30)

into the societal structure of eighteenth-century European societies.

PUBLIC SPHERE AND PRIVATE REALM

It is important to understand that by "private realm" Habermas does not only mean intimate bonds between partners, family members, or friends, as one might presume from our contemporary usage of the word. The private realm is called private because it is "private citizens" who act in it as opposed to bearers of public authority and state functions. In this private realm we find entrepreneurs, merchants, and craftsmen ("civil society") as well as families with male patriarchs, subordinate wives, and often domestic servants (the "conjugal family's internal space"). These social categories and activities are increasingly separated from the state (public administration, police, army) and from the noble court in which members of the aristocracy still led privileged lives in the eighteenth century. To the degree that private citizens discovered their interest in emancipating themselves from the aristocracy and claiming leading roles in the newly emerging capitalist society, a separate "public sphere" developed. It consisted of coffee houses, salons, intellectual debate circles, print periodicals, buyers and sellers of books, journals, and works of art as well as concert- and theater-goers ("town").

In the early phase of the transition from feudalism to capitalism, the public sphere was more confined to discussing literary matters and developing specifically bourgeois tastes that differentiated it from salon conversation and art-making in the noble courts. This initial "public sphere in the world of letters" or "cultural public sphere," as it was later called, became more politicized when the new bourgeois class asserted itself also as the leading stratum in matters of politics and governance. The emerging "public sphere in the political realm" (or "political public sphere") started to assume its role as an intermediary sphere between state and citizens – a role still familiar in democratic-capitalist countries today.

State actions became the object of criticism and reflection more often and the interests of private citizens came to be voiced more clearly vis-à-vis noble rulers and aristocrats. The political public sphere became a critical counterpart of state authority and challenged unjustified privileges and political oppression more explicitly. It did so by forming and circulating "public opinions" through discussion that ultimately challenged the feudal state and led to the development of democratic institutions. To organize and professionalize such discussion, political journalism evolved as a profession during the nineteenth century. The center of public life was no longer to be found in the noble court, but in the "town" located opposite the feudal palace, where an independent and self-conscious bourgeois life developed (Habermas 1989a, 30).

The public sphere in the eighteenth century is both a product and a driving force of societal differentiation. It is called "bourgeois" because it is inextricably linked to the rise of bourgeois society, a form of society in which the land- and money-owning classes assume the leading role in the polity – and push the formerly dominant aristocracy to the side. Bourgeois society developed in Europe in the eighteenth and nineteenth centuries, somewhat earlier in Britain and France than in Germany, where dozens of more or less independent small-scale principalities slowed down the transformation considerably. Bourgeois society is characterized by a differentiation of three roles that people play in society (and these roles are more clearly differentiated in the French language than in English or German): the *bourgeois* acting in his own interest on markets for goods and labor; the *citoyen* who determines his own fate by forming and expressing opinions and participating politically (through protesting, petitioning, voting, etc.); and the *homme*, the "private man" enmeshed in a web of personal relations with his wife, children, relatives, and friends. The use of the male pronoun and the allusion to heterosexual partnership here is in no way accidental; we will return to the gendered character of the bourgeois public sphere later.

The rise and fall of the public sphere:
How Habermas builds his argument
In his book *Structural transformation of the public sphere* Jürgen Habermas develops his argument in twenty-five chapters that are grouped into seven larger sections. Section I comprises three chapters in which Habermas establishes his basic understanding of the bourgeois public sphere and describes its emancipation from the earlier feudal type of "representative publicness." Representative publicness denotes the feudal ruler's "display of inherent spiritual power or dignity before an audience" (translator's

note in Habermas 1989a, xv). According to Habermas, this mode of public display was superseded by "critical publicity" as the dominant mode in which the bourgeois public sphere addresses the state.

With this basic idea in hand Habermas proceeds to treat three large themes that characterize the bourgeois public sphere both historically and theoretically: the social structures underlying the public sphere (section II), its political functions (section III), and the ideas and ideologies that characterize and legitimize the bourgeois public sphere (section IV). By "social structures" Habermas means, as we have seen in figure 1.1, the way material production and the production of cultural goods, including the emerging media system, are organized. "Political functions" captures the contestatory relations that discussions in the literary and political public spheres establish vis-à-vis state authorities and the policies they issue. Under "ideas and ideologies" Habermas discusses the history of eighteenth- and nineteenth-century philosophy about what should be the purpose of public discussion and public opinion, which co-evolved with the actual rise of the public sphere itself.

In the following sections (V to VII) of the book, Habermas then describes what he sees as the degenerative transformation or demise of the bourgeois public sphere during the late nineteenth and twentieth centuries. In doing so, he uses exactly the same three argumentative perspectives: He first analyzes the social-structural transformation of the public sphere (section V) and diagnoses a mutual infiltration of the formerly separated spheres of public authority and private life through the establishment of powerful commercial associations and political parties that position themselves above the deliberating *citoyens*. In section VI Habermas describes the transformation of the public sphere's political functions as a shift from critical publicity to "manufactured publicity" directed at securing mass loyalty rather than critical, bottom-up discussion. In section VII, finally, he offers a reflection of the ideology of that transformed public sphere, which he detects in the "social-psychological liquidation" of the original, discussion-based concept of public opinion in the emerging practice of opinion polling.

The parallel, threefold organization that Habermas uses to tell the tale of both the emergence and the degeneration of the bourgeois public sphere gives the book coherence and clarity – despite the complexity of its subject matter and the density of its language. Note, however, that throughout the book, the term "public sphere" is used in both a historical-empirical and a critical-normative sense. Historically, Habermas sees the evolution of the public sphere as a process of degeneration. But normatively, he emphasizes the continuing timeliness and necessity of the critical ideal of inclusive, rational, and undistorted discussion that he associates with the original bourgeois forms of public communication in coffee houses and journals (see Fraser 2009).

THE MEDIA OF THE EARLY BOURGEOIS PUBLIC SPHERE

What kind of media supported the early forms of the bourgeois public sphere? Habermas mentions different types of periodicals. For one, journals devoted to art and cultural criticism emerged in the eighteenth century as a forum in which the philosophy, literature, and art of the day were discussed by erudite men (and occasionally women). According to Habermas (1989a, 42) these journals served as catalysts in the process by which the educated urban classes developed a sense of their commonalities and historical mission as an enlightened public. Small, local debate circles and informal conversations began to be connected translocally because people started reading the same periodicals and discussing similar matters and trends in different locales. In this way the bourgeois public emerged.

Apart from the journals of cultural criticism Habermas points to the importance of the "moral weeklies," which discussed matters of manners and morals: "charities and schools for the poor, the improvement of education, pleas for civilized forms of conduct, polemics against the vices of gambling, fanaticism, and pedantry and against the tasteless-ness of the aesthetes and the eccentricities of the learned" (Habermas 1989a, 43). These weeklies "worked toward the spread of tolerance, the emancipation of civic morality from moral theology and of practical wisdom from the philosophy of the scholars. The public that read and debated this sort of thing read and debated about itself" (p. 43).

Reading and debating were elements of the same process:

> The periodical articles were not only made the object of dis-
> cussion by the public of the coffee houses but were viewed
> as integral parts of this discussion; this was demonstrated by
> the flood of letters from which the editor each week pub-
> lished a selection. When the *Spectator* separated from the
> *Guardian* [two British periodicals founded in 1711 and 1713]
> the letters to the editor were provided with a special insti-
> tution: on the west side of Button's Coffee House a lion's
> head was attached through whose jaws the reader threw his
> letter. The dialogue form too, employed by many of the arti-
> cles, attested to their proximity to the spoken word. One and
> the same discussion transposed into a different medium was
> continued in order to reenter, via reading, the original con-
> versational medium. (Habermas 1989a, 42)

In this passage Habermas offers a vivid account of how exactly a public emerged through the exchange of ideas – and how this formation was mediated very early on. The media involved at the time were print periodicals with a special emphasis on letters to the editor, and the process closely integrated mediated and face-to-face exchanges. The formation of a public by interactive communication between professional communicators and engaged members of their audience is not unlike some processes observed today in the blogosphere or in comment sections online. It signifies a basic constituent element in the functioning of a public sphere and has inspired many contemporary communication researchers to interpret online discussion as instances of public spheres (see chapter 5 for more details).

THE ALLEGED DEMISE OF THE PUBLIC SPHERE

Habermas offers a developmental account of the bourgeois public sphere leading from its peak period in the late eighteenth and early nineteenth centuries to its disintegration into "manufactured publicity" during the late nineteenth and twentieth centuries. This account offers a very bold claim that essentially rests on Habermas's strong idealization of the early bourgeois public sphere and its subsequent juxtaposition with what he perceived as a gravely deficient reality at the place and time of his writing, namely postwar Germany in the late 1950s and early 1960s. Interestingly, in this account, crucial elements of the communications industry as we know it today – mass media, the public relations and advertising industries, and public opinion polling – are precisely seen as symptoms of the *decay* of critical publicity identified as the hallmark of the earlier bourgeois public sphere. How is this possible?

During the first half of the nineteenth century, the older form of journalism performed by individual writers who acted as their own publishers was increasingly replaced by two new forms of publishing: commercial newspapers addressing large portions of a public while refraining from explicit political stances, and a party press in which newspapers became the mouthpieces of political organizations. In both cases editors were employed, rather than self-employed, and increasingly subject to directives rather than autonomous decision-makers (Habermas 1989a, 186). Commercial newspapers were financed by advertising and thus started selling two commodities at the same time: advertising space was sold to businesses, and the editorial section in which the advertisements were embedded was sold to its readers (Bücher as quoted in Habermas 1989a, 184). "[I]n the measure that the public sphere became a field for business advertising, private people as owners of private property [the *bourgeois*, as defined earlier] had a direct effect on private people as the public [the *citoyens*]" (Habermas 1989a, 189). In Habermas's view this polluted the critical, self-empowering discussions between citizens by inserting into the realm of public communication the particularistic interests of producers and consumers of commercial goods and services, thus distracting participants from focusing on the issues important to all.

But the critical public sphere of debating citizens was polluted not only by its marriage with private economic activity in the form of advertising. Much the same can be said, according to Habermas's diagnosis, about political public relations. "Publicity work is aimed at strengthening the prestige of one's own position without making the matter on which the compromise is to be achieved itself a topic of *public discussion*. Organizations and functionaries display *representation*" (Habermas 1989a, 200). This circumvention of public discussion on the part of political organizations and their representatives fundamentally alters the character of the entire process of public communication. The public sphere is "refeudalized" in the sense that public communication is performed in front of an audience rather than enacted by the members of that audience.

> The aura of personally represented authority returns as an aspect of publicity; to this extent modern publicity indeed has affinity with feudal publicity. Public relations do not genuinely concern public opinion but opinion in the sense of reputation. The public sphere becomes the court *before* which public prestige can be displayed – rather than *in* which critical debate is carried on. (Habermas 1989a, 200f.)

Habermas juxtaposes here true public opinion as generated through debate between active citizens and "opinion in the sense of reputation," that is, opinions that contain approval or disapproval of public figures and their plans and actions, which are manufactured by top-down public relations activities but not generated through bottom-up discussion. These manufactured opinions are labeled "nonpublic" exactly because no process of public exchange produces them. A final element in the demise of the bourgeois public sphere, which Habermas diagnoses, thus concerns the rise of opinion polling during the twentieth century. Opinion polls record nonpublic opinions; that is, they register what people think irrespective of whether a discussion has taken place. They also register opinions only in relation to issues that the polling organizations find interesting irrespective of whether they mirror the actual concerns of citizens. And through their mere existence polling results exert an influence on political decision-makers that in Habermas's eyes was formerly legitimately reserved for the results of critical debates (Habermas 1989a, 220). The routine of recording existing nonpublic opinions in opinion polls amounts to a "social-psychological liquidation" of the older, more demanding concept of discussion-based public opinion (Habermas 1989a, 236). The demise of the public sphere is thus closely linked in Habermas's account to the rise of the modern communications industry and the disjunction of that industry from the normative notion of a public sphere predicated on rational-critical debate. In the new realm of manufactured publicity, Habermas concludes, citizens are not generators but mere addressees of communication, only strategically used to secure mass loyalty and mass consumption. Importantly, in his "Further reflections on the public sphere" Habermas (1992) makes decisive revisions to this rather gloomy narrative of decay.

> In fine, my diagnosis of a unilinear development from a politically active public to one withdrawn into a bad privacy, from a "culture-debating to a culture-consuming public," is too simplistic. At the time, I was too pessimistic about the resisting power and above all the critical potential of a pluralistic, internally much differentiated mass public whose cultural usages have begun to shake off the constraints of class. In conjunction with the ambivalent relaxation of the distinction between high and low culture, and the no less ambiguous "new intimacy between culture and politics," which is more complex than a mere assimilation of information to entertainment, the standards of evaluation themselves have also changed. (Habermas 1992, 438f.)

Habermas now approvingly refers to Stuart Hall's (1980) three modes of reception, namely the affirmative, the critical, and the negotiated modes, which direct attention to the possibilities for resistance to that manufactured publicity that Habermas still dreads. This also means that the mass-mediated arena of public communication now appears as a battleground between bottom-up discussion and top-down persuasion. With this move Habermas also leaves behind the profound pessimism of the first generation of the Frankfurt School, as exemplified in Adorno and Horkheimer's chapter on the "Culture Industry" in their *Dialectic of enlightenment* (Adorno and Horkheimer 2002; originally published in German in 1947), according to which standardized cultural products lead to passivity and uncritical acceptance of domination. By the early 1990s Habermas's verdict on these matters has become much less fixed than it had been three decades before. But his normative preference for free-floating, bottom-up discussion still stands. It clearly motivates his move in the 1990s toward a comprehensive consideration of what it means for a democracy to be "deliberative" (Habermas 1996) and of how a public sphere can be conceived that is adequate for today's complex societies (see chapter 3).

A PUBLIC SPHERE OF AFFLUENT WHITE MALES? SOCIAL EXCLUSION AND ITS CRITICS

The gloomy tone of Habermas's original demise narrative is only the flipside of an overly rosy picture of the original bourgeois public sphere. And so his idealized notion of the bourgeois variant has been subject to severe criticism by other scholars. Some critics have pointed to his neglect of non-bourgeois public spheres: the plebeian or proletarian public spheres developing in the workplace and permeating public communication since the Industrial Revolution in Europe (Negt and Kluge 1972). Others have emphasized that the confinement of women to the private realm in the early bourgeois period devalues the supposedly rational discussions among equals (Fraser 1992). It is quite clear that the emancipation of the bourgeois class in the emerging bourgeois public sphere of the eighteenth and nineteenth centuries is traded off against the exclusion of women and the poor from that same public sphere. The fact that Habermas based his idealization on this type of *exclusionary emancipation* of the bourgeois male rightly provoked criticism.

Habermas was at least half-conscious of this shortcoming of his account. In his preface to the first (German-language) edition of *Structural transformation of the public sphere*, published in 1962, Habermas already expressed a reservation with respect to the scope of his analysis.

> Our investigation is limited to the structure and function of the *liberal* model of the bourgeois public sphere, to its emergence and transformation. Thus it refers to those features of a historical constellation that attained dominance and leaves aside the plebeian public sphere as a variant that in a sense was suppressed in the historical process. [...] Yet even this *plebeian* public sphere, whose continued but submerged existence manifested itself in the Chartist Movement and especially in the anarchist tradition of the workers' movement on the continent, remains oriented toward the intentions of the bourgeois public sphere. [...] Precisely for this reason it must be strictly distinguished form the plebiscitary-acclamatory form of the regimented public sphere characterizing dictatorships in highly developed industrial societies. (Habermas 1989a, xviii)

This quote, originally written in post-World War II Germany, distinguishes rebellious forms of radical opposition to the emerging capitalist system (plebeian public sphere) from the managed and coercive forms of publicity found at his time of writing and until 1989 in the "real-socialist" societies of Eastern Europe and the Soviet Union. With respect to the latter, Habermas's analysis does provide the necessary critical edge. And it is no wonder, therefore, that many Eastern European observers valued his *Structural transformation of the public sphere* as an aid in understanding both the nature of Communist rule and the transformations of their societies after the end of the Cold War. But with respect to the former, the historical suppression of the plebeian public sphere, and its subsequent theoretical suppression in Habermas's theory, his 1962 book idealized the bourgeois public sphere in unwarranted and unnecessary fashion.

Habermas did respond to his social-exclusion critics by distinguishing two forms of social exclusion in his "Further reflections on the public sphere" (Habermas 1992). A less severe form pertains to social groups, particularly the working class, whose interests and concerns are pushed to the side by the protagonists of the bourgeois public sphere. But plebeian and proletarian forms of public expression have existed both alongside and intertwined with the bourgeois public sphere from its beginnings (Habermas 1992, 426). This form of social exclusion can therefore be redressed within the parameters of the bourgeois public sphere. The workers' movement has become an integral and vibrant part of democratic contestation in the political public sphere over the course of the nineteenth and twentieth centuries by partly developing autonomous arenas of self-identification and reflection and partly permeating dominant, bourgeois debates.

The second, more fundamental form of social exclusion pertains to women. At the beginning of the 1990s Habermas concedes that the exclusion of women was *constitutive* for the character of the bourgeois public sphere. Women were confined to the "conjugal family's internal space" (see figure 1.1), which was by definition removed from, and construed as the "other" of, discussion in the public sphere. This expulsion of women's lifeworlds, experiences, and interests from the original bourgeois public sphere, Habermas contends (1992, 429), could only be redressed by a transformation in which the bourgeois public sphere changed its character. Only by abolishing the constructed separation of the public and private spheres and the subsequent inclusion of formerly "private" matters (e.g., the confinement of women to unpaid labor; domestic violence; sexual exploitation; etc.) in more encompassing public debates could women become emancipated (Fraser 1992). But Habermas emphasizes that the bourgeois public sphere did exhibit a potential for feminist self-transformation: The universalistic premises of the discourses in the bourgeois public sphere could always be directed at these discourses themselves precisely because they were couched in universalistic terms. From the 1960s the bourgeois public sphere was forced to self-transform and acknowledge that what had formerly been excluded from it as private matters are now public matters to be openly discussed.

Of course, social exclusion is an undeniable fact of most public discourse to this day. Some social actors do not possess enough resources to be able to enter public debate, be it because they do not have enough time, or money, or cultural competencies. In fact, public deliberation is often highly stratified (Peters 2008e). Social exclusion reduces the possible range of perspectives present in public debate and thus constitutes an obstacle to genuinely inclusive public exchanges. Habermas has acknowledged in his writing the existence of social exclusion and its problematic character for rational-critical democratic debate. The main point of difference between Habermas and his "exclusion critics" is whether the power structures that lead to social exclusion are "always there," unavoidable and ever-present, or whether, as Habermas contends, exclusion can be redressed through self-transformation in order to come closer to the ideal version of public debate. Habermas sees the successive inclusion of women, workers, racial or immigrant minorities, people with non-mainstream sexual orientations, etc. in the history of the public sphere as historical achievements that have improved conditions for meaningful, inclusive public debate in the long run. And he is certainly sympathetic to attempts to further open up debates, for example by including the voices of the European and global periphery in public debates in the center. Considering Habermas's revisions and rejoinders and the general thrust of his argument, the social inclusion line of criticism, therefore, does not really find its mark in his work any more today.

SUMMARY

Looking back at Habermas's early theory of the public sphere (1962) and its international reception following the publication of the English translation in 1989, two issues stand out. One has to do with the overly pessimistic picture that Habermas paints of the role of the media in public debate in the twentieth century; the other pertains to his overly optimistic view of the public exchanges in coffee houses and salons among *citoyens* in the nineteenth century.

First, we have seen that Habermas held no high opinion of the mass media of his time – especially newspapers and radio; television was only just emerging as a mass medium at the time of his writing – in terms of the critical rationality he envisioned for public debate. These media seemed to him to be agents of the "refeudalization" of the public sphere, agents of top-down, manipulative management of representative publicity. They seemed to stifle critical engagement among citizens and between them and the economic and political power-holders. Habermas partly revoked this pessimism himself, as we have seen. But it also gave rise to a program of empirical investigation interested in what exactly we can expect from the various types of mass and network media if we use Habermas's idea of critical rationality as a yardstick. We will look at these investigations in detail in chapters 5 and 6.

The second issue concerns Habermas's overly optimistic account of the emerging bourgeois public sphere. As we have seen, this idealizing view was essentially built on more or less uncritically accepting the exclusionary nature of the emancipation of the bourgeois class in public discussions in the eighteenth and nineteenth centuries. Consequently, Habermas ascribed to the bourgeois public sphere a critical rationality that may not always have existed historically and that, to the extent that it did exist, was achieved at the expense of relegating other subordinated groups to invisibility and muteness. Does this mean that we have to discard this notion of critical rationality altogether in order to do justice to the rights of those subordinated groups? Or can these groups somehow be included in the public sphere and the principle of critical rationality be upheld? These probing questions have given rise to two innovations in public sphere theory and Habermas's own contributions to that field. One innovation is associated with the concept of "counterpublics" and Habermas's recognition in his later book *Between facts and norms* (1996, 372) that the public sphere is not monolithic, but a network of diverse publics. We will return to this point when we look at that book in chapter 3; and we will take up the issue of counterpublics in chapter 7 in greater detail. The other innovation reflects Habermas's interest in clarifying the sources of rationality in human life and in society *without* recourse to a particular group – the bourgeois class – or historical period. We will review this attempt at a general theory of communicative rationality in the next chapter.

RECOMMENDED READING

Fraser, N. (1992) "Rethinking the public sphere: A contribution to the critique of actually existing democracy." In: Calhoun, C. (ed.) *Habermas and the public sphere.* MIT Press, Cambridge, MA, pp. 109–42.

Habermas, J. (1992) "Further reflections on the public sphere." In: Calhoun, C. (ed.) *Habermas and the public sphere.* MIT Press, Cambridge, MA, pp. 421–61.

Peters, B. (2008e) "The meaning of the public sphere." In: Wessler, H. (ed.) *Public deliberation and public culture: The writings of Bernhard Peters, 1993–2005.* Palgrave Macmillan, London, pp. 33–67.

2

NURTURING COMMUNICATIVE ACTION

In his early book on the *Structural transformation of the public sphere* Habermas was not yet able to specify exactly the origin of the rationalizing power of argumentative exchange that he saw in the coffee houses and journals of the eighteenth and early nineteenth centuries. How exactly does reason enter human life and society? In his magnum opus, *The theory of communicative action* Habermas (1984; 1987b) now attempts to fundamentally clarify this question. In doing so, he also builds a new theoretical foundation for his thinking about communication and the media. Even though the media do not feature prominently in this two-volume work, the basic theoretical tenets developed here have a direct bearing on how Habermas sees the media.

Theorizing communicative action:
How Habermas builds his argument
The *Theory of communicative action* comprises two volumes (Habermas 1984; 1987b). In both volumes Habermas

develops his wide-ranging argument in response to other important social scientists and philosophers spanning the history of ideas from the eighteenth to the twentieth centuries. Important counterparts and sources of inspiration include Immanuel Kant, Karl Marx, Emile Durkheim, Max Weber, George Herbert Mead, Talcott Parsons, John Austin, and Karl Popper, among others. These deep examinations of both Habermas's precursors and theoretical rivals are interrupted, however, by two long chapters called "Intermediate reflections," which synthesize the thrust of his argument in a more self-contained and condensed fashion. In the first such chapter, "Intermediate reflections: Social action, purposive activity, and communication" (chapter III, pp. 273–337 of volume 1), Habermas develops his theory of human action and juxtaposes his conception of communicative action with other forms, particularly strategic action.

In the second such chapter, "Intermediate reflections: System and lifeworld" (chapter VI, pp. 113–97 of volume 2), Habermas theorizes society as a whole and develops his distinction between lifeworld and system. The media are initially conceived as a part of the lifeworld in which people make sense of their lives and the world by engaging in communicative action. But as the lifeworld is in danger of being colonized by the imperatives of the economic and political systems, the media, too, are prone to be instrumentalized by economic and political power-holders, according to Habermas.

Apart from the two "Intermediate reflections," a few other passages in the *Theory of communicative action* are particularly important. Chapter I.3 (Habermas 1984, 75–101), "Relations to the world and aspects of rationality in four sociological concepts of action," develops communicative action in relation to three other conceptions of human action (i.e., teleological, normatively regulated, and dramaturgical action) and thus lays the groundwork for Habermas's theory. And in the concluding chapter of volume 2, "The tasks of a critical theory of society," in the very brief section "(c) Mass media and mass culture" (Habermas 1987b, 389–91) Habermas revises his earlier evaluation of the mass media as manipulative by briefly alluding to more nuanced accounts found in communication and cultural studies scholarship at the time of his writing (the late 1970s).

COMMUNICATIVE ACTION: THEORIZING HUMAN ACTIVITY

In answering the rationality question Habermas begins in volume 1 of the *Theory of communicative action* on the micro level of individual human actions. At this stage he does not look at social formations or groups such as journalists, politicians, or the public at large. Nor does he study societal domains such as the public and private spheres, or civil society and state institutions. He returns to these meso and macro phenomena later, in volume 2. But initially, human actions are his object of study. In order to clarify the foundations of rationality Habermas asks: What is required for people to agree with each other? And he essentially needs three argumentative steps to answer that question.

Step 1: Habermas distinguishes between rationally motivated agreement and other forms of agreement. Someone can agree to someone else simply because she is forced to, i.e. because disagreement would yield negative consequences. Or someone can agree to what someone else is saying simply out of tacit conformity, without actually testing the merit of what was being said. Rationally motivated agreement, however, is different. When we agree with someone on a rational basis we actively and consciously accept the communicative offer made by our counterpart (Habermas 1984, 302). But what exactly do we accept when we agree with someone in this rational way?

Step 2: We accept, Habermas contends, three different validity claims that the other person has implicitly made when they talked to us. That other person has implicitly claimed that (a) what they have said was true, (b) what they have said conforms to generally acceptable social norms, and (c) their utterance reflected their true intentions. In other words, that person has made the validity claims of truth, (moral) rightness, and sincerity or truthfulness (Habermas 1984, 307). By agreeing with that person in a rationally motivated way we accept these validity claims, that is, we are prepared to assume that, if tested, the other person would be able to give convincing reasons for why we should believe them. The three validity claims do not have to be justified all the time – otherwise, smooth interaction would be impossible. Instead we work on the assumption that they could be redeemed if necessary. But why do we make and accept these and only these validity claims when we communicate with others?

Step 3: The three validity claims are not arbitrary inventions and do not fall from heaven. They relate, Habermas says, to the three worlds in which we live as humans:

1 The objective world (as the totality of all entities about which true statements are possible);
2 The social world (as the totality of all legitimately regulated interpersonal relations);
3 The subjective world (as the totality of the experiences of the speaker to which he has privileged access). (Habermas 1984, 100)

When we speak we relate to all three worlds simultaneously by making validity claims about them: We claim truth with respect to the objective world, moral rightness with respect to the social relationships in which our speaking is embedded, and sincerity or truthfulness with respect to our inner world. With these three steps we now know what it means to agree with someone in a rationally motivated way, or in other words, what it means to reach understanding. Communicative action is "action oriented to reaching understanding" and as such it is diametrically opposed to strategic action, that is, "action oriented to success" (Habermas 1984, 286) (see table 2.1). In success-oriented action we try to move somebody in our direction without their rationally motivated agreement. We can do this openly or in a concealed fashion. In open strategic action we have two options: We can either threaten someone into complying with our intentions or we can offer incentives. Either way rational agreement is neither intended nor necessary. Threats and incentives are well-known instruments in negotiations.

Concealed strategic communication is a bit more complicated. "In situations of concealed strategic action, at least one of the parties behaves with an orientation to success, but leaves others to believe that all the presuppositions of communicative action are satisfied" (Habermas 1984, 332). If the communicating party consciously deceives *others* about his or her strategic intentions, he or she manipulates these others. The resulting surreptitious agreement breaks down as soon as the manipulation is exposed. In the second variant of concealed strategic action the communicating party even deceives himself or herself about the fact that they have abandoned the orientation to reaching understanding for an orientation to success. This type of self-deception can be based in neuroticism (e.g., the speaker is unaware of his or her own defense mechanisms against repressed conflicts) or

Table 2.1 Types of communication and agreement (adapted from Burkart and Lang 2007, 47)

Type of communication		Mechanism through which actions are coordinated	Type of agreement achieved
1 Communication oriented to understanding		Shared interpretations	Rationally motivated agreement
2 Strategic communication	2a Openly strategic communication	2ai Threats 2aii Incentives	Coerced agreement Bought agreement
	2b Concealed strategic communication	2bi Conscious deception (= Manipulation)	Surreptitious agreement
		2bii Unconscious deception (= Systematically distorted communication)	Illusory agreement

an ideological stance immunized against counter-arguments (e.g., the speaker rationalizes their own dominant position vis-à-vis subaltern groups as natural and uses language that conceals the relation of dominance, such as "colorblind talk" in the context of the USA; Huspek 2007b, 362). In both cases, communication is systematically distorted and the resulting agreement is based on an illusion of mutual understanding (Habermas 1984, 332f.; see also Burkart and Lang 2007, 46). From this description of the different types of communication it becomes clear that communicative action, with its orientation to reaching understanding through rationally motivated agreement, is the normatively most desirable form of communication.

FROM INDIVIDUAL COMMUNICATION
TO TYPES OF DISCOURSES

Communicative action is not something that only goes on between two people. While dyadic communication is the prototype of all communication, Habermas's conception of communicative action already implies larger social formations. For one, communicative action serves to coordinate individual action in chains and webs of actions. The coordination of action is a fundamental problem that every social formation and every society must solve. As we have seen, to communicate with an orientation to reaching understanding means to presuppose that the validity claims that the speaker makes could be redeemed if necessary. Through this presupposition the action of the addressee is already bound to the speaker's action. The addressee either accepts the validity claims of truth, rightness, and truthfulness or challenges one or more of these claims. In the first case the communicative action chain can continue with a reciprocal speech act by the addressee; in the second the addressee engages in specific types of discourses that serve to problematize validity claims. In both cases, a cooperative process of interpretation ensues through which actors coordinate their actions (Habermas 1984, 151). In addition, in processes of mutual understanding the actors develop a reflexive relation to the world, i.e. they account for the fact that the validity of their utterances can be contested and that they might be called upon to justify their validity claims (Habermas 1984, 148).

If the addressee does not accept one or more of the validity claims, two reactions are possible in the process of communicative action, namely simple repairs or discourses. To elicit *simple repairs*, the addressee can ask questions like: "Is it really as you are saying?" (truth), "Were you allowed to do this?" (rightness), or "Are you deceiving me, or even yourself?" (truthfulness). The speaker can respond with measures of simple repair: With respect to the truth claim she can develop assertions and explanations; to repair the rightness claim she can advance justifications for the legitimacy of her actions; and in response to challenges of her sincerity or truthfulness she – can actually do nothing by way of simple repair. In contrast to truth and rightness, claims to sincerity or truthfulness can be resolved not by the person whose sincerity is being questioned, but only by third parties (Habermas 1989b, 111). In cases of doubt about sincerity, therefore, the addressee is well advised to turn to others rather than to the speaker to regain certainty – or to wait and see whether in the long run the consequences of the speaker's action conform to what she professed (Habermas 1984, 41).

If, however, the addressee cannot be brought to accept the validity claims he deems problematic even after simple repair, he can demand that the speaker fully redeem her validity claim by advancing those reasons that have hitherto been presupposed. Exchanges of arguments that advance or refute precisely such reasons are called *discourses*. Discourses in which speakers try to resolve problematic truth claims are called "theoretical discourses," and discourses in which rightness claims are resolved are called "practical discourses" (Habermas 1984, 19). Again, for problematic sincerity claims no argumentative redemption by the same speaker exists, so no discourse between speaker and addressee can help here.

Media content is full of both theoretical and practical discourses. One example of a theoretical discourse concerns knowledge about the manmade nature of global climate change. The traditional interpretation that climate variations are due to natural processes alone is strongly challenged by the now overwhelming scientific consensus that human activity has contributed greatly – through industrialization and the burning of fossil fuels – to the surge in average temperatures over the past centuries. Note that truth claims are to be problematized and resolved on the basis of available facts, not on what has been called "truthiness" in the US context, that is, the perception that something "feels true." Public debate infused with "truthiness" is the opposite of theoretical discourse. Thus, denying the anthropogenic nature of climate change because it does not "feel true" or because it is said to be a "hoax" rather than through the use of accepted scientific knowledge does not constitute theoretical discourse, and is thus not an instance of communication oriented to understanding.

An example of a practical discourse would be the debate about the permissibility of abortions (see Ferree et al. 2002). Is it justifiable to abort a fetus, and if so, why? Conversely, why should it be justifiable to curtail a woman's right to decide about her body? In the process of exchanging arguments on these questions, it may well be that speakers advance qualifications in the form of: "Yes, it is OK to abort a fetus if the woman so desires, but only until week 12 of her pregnancy." Or: "No, it is generally not OK, but in a specific case the permission of a medical doctor or a religious authority can legitimate an abortion." Practical discourses are often difficult. The example shows that practical discourses may refer to issues about which people deeply disagree, and that may even involve contradictory values both of which have strong merits and plausibility for most discourse participants. In culturally heterogeneous societies – and most societies are, in fact, heterogeneous under the conditions of globalization – most practical discourses will not end in consensus, but remain substantively unresolved. This is why, in Habermas's view, it is all the more important that they be conducted without coercion, ignorance, and deception, that is, without the usual elements of strategic action.

To identify the kind of communication needed for theoretical and practical discourses, Habermas had developed the ideal speech situation as a *thought experiment* in a paper on theories of truth published in German in 1972. An ideal speech situation would be devoid of all external and internal pressures and constraints. External constraints pertain to the lack of knowledge and time, and the use of intimidation and deception. Internal constraints are distortions of the chance to be heard, which is supposed to be equal among all participants. If all of these external and internal constraints were absent, Habermas contends, discourse participants would exercise "no force except that of the better argument" (Habermas 1975, 108; see 1989b, 116).

The idea of an ideal speech situation in which the unforced force of the better argument can reign is often associated automatically with Habermas's name. Ironically, he himself never used it again after 1972. In addition, the ideal speech situation was never meant as a *model* that should be implemented in real life (see Habermas 1996, 322) but as a summary of the necessary pragmatic presuppositions that speakers must make when they argue seriously. These presuppositions then serve a *regulative idea* that invites us all to move our behavior in the direction of the ideal when we discuss – even though we are aware that we do not fully live up to the ideal. The distinction between an ideal model and a regulative idea based on unavoidable presuppositions is important, because the regulative idea can exert its stimulating influence on speakers' behavior under less than ideal conditions also and is thus more valuable for the analysis of real-world discussion contexts.

LIFEWORLD AND SYSTEM: THEORIZING SOCIETAL TOTALITY

But what does all of this have to do with the media and mediated public spheres? In order to show how validity claims and discourses are related to macro institutions such as politics and the media, Habermas develops two extensive arguments in volume 2 of his *Theory of communicative action* (Habermas 1987b). In a first step he asks: Where do those norms come from that people invoke when they make validity claims of moral rightness and that are contested in practical discourse? And where do our presuppositions about the objective world come from that we take for granted when we make truth claims? Both norms and knowledge about the world are resources that must be available to people in order for them to engage in communication oriented to reaching understanding. Thus communicative action presupposes and reproduces a supra-individual context from which people can draw these resources. This context is what Habermas calls "lifeworld," and it will be important to understand what he means by this term.

In a second argumentative step Habermas then juxtaposes this "lifeworld" with "systems." Habermas is interested primarily in the systems of administrative power, i.e. the political system, and the economic system. Systems are social macro structures that are not dependent on communicative action to function and to be reproduced over time. Both are reproduced by norm-free functional imperatives and steered by symbolically generalized steering media. These steering media have nothing to do with the media of mass and interpersonal communication that we have looked at so far. Rather they are means by which actions in the political or the economic system are coordinated *without* recourse to language or even mutual understanding. Politics is steered by power, the economy by money, that is, by monetary incentives. Money, for example, connects the action of a seller of goods with the action of a buyer by providing a common reference point that ensures the commensurability of the two actions. The same is true for politics. All actions in politics are primarily about attaining or securing power, about who constitutes the government and who is in the opposition, about who is winning an election, a parliamentary vote, or a referendum. All actions in the political world can be assessed as to what they mean for the distribution of power, and thereby they are mutually coordinated (Habermas 1987b, 274).

Essentially, Habermas proposes theorizing society in two different but complementary ways. Society can be looked at from the "perspective of acting subjects as the *lifeworld of a social group*. In contrast, from the observer's perspective of someone not involved, society can be conceived only as a *system of actions* such that each action has a functional significance according to its contribution to the maintenance of the system" (Habermas 1987b, 117). Lifeworld and system are not simply different "things" in the social world. Rather they become visible only from different vantage points, namely the participant's perspective in the case of the lifeworld and the observer's perspective in the case of the system.

Following a participant's perspective means that the lifeworld always appears as the *lifeworld of somebody*, of a concrete historical collective. It is the world that the members of that collective take for granted and presuppose in their actions. In concrete situations a part of that unquestioned background is being highlighted and delimited as a "field of actual needs for mutual understanding and of actual options for action" (Habermas 1987b, 123). The lifeworld of a concrete collective thus both constitutes the *context* for communicative action and furnishes *resources* to be used in situations.

In fact, Habermas distinguishes three types of resources that are provided by the lifeworld: (a) a repository of cultural knowledge, (b) the values and norms of the respective collective, and (c) individual competencies acquired in socialization and learning processes. These three types of resources can actually be conceived as three structural components of the lifeworld, namely culture, society, and personality.

> I call *culture* the store of knowledge from which those engaged in communicative action draw interpretations susceptible of consensus as they come to an understanding about something in the world. I call *society* (in the narrower sense of a component of the lifeworld) the legitimate orders from which those engaged in communicative action gather a solidarity, based on belonging to groups, as they enter into interpersonal relationships with each other. *Personality* serves as a term of art for acquired competencies that render a subject capable of speech and action and hence able to participate in processes of mutual understanding in a given context and to maintain his own identity in the shifting contexts of interaction. (Habermas 1987a, 343)

Table 2.2 summarizes the three structural components. It is important to note that Habermas locates the cultural and the political public spheres at the heart of a collective's lifeworld. They constitute central social spaces in which cultural

Table 2.2 Components of the lifeworld and their reproduction (based on Habermas 1987b, 142–6)

	Culture	Society	Personality
Reproduction processes	Cultural reproduction	Social integration	Socialization
Primary reproductive function of communicative action	Transmission, critique, and acquisition of cultural knowledge	Coordination of actions via intersubjectively recognized validity claims	Formation of identity
Contribution of reproduction processes to maintaining the lifeworld	Interpretive schemes fit for consensus ("valid knowledge")	Legitimately ordered interpersonal relations, group-based solidarity	Interactive capabilities ("personal identity")
Disturbances to which reproduction processes react	Loss of meaning	Anomie (loss of social order, alienation)	Psychopathologies
Social space for reproduction processes	Cultural public sphere	Political public sphere	Private sphere
Action systems specialized in reproduction processes	Science, religion, art, cultural communication media	Democratic politics (discursive will-formation), law, political news and discussion media	Education

traditions and conceptions of the public good can be probed, maintained, and developed. Crucially, their placing in the lifeworld also means that they are conceived as carriers of communication oriented to mutual understanding, not as mere conduits for strategic communication by political or economic actors or as sites in which the functional imperatives of politics and business reign exclusively. In Habermas's view, public spheres are rooted in the informal interactions of the lifeworld, and this connection to the lifeworld must be defended against purely functional imperatives, that is, against the influence of power and money. In his later book *Between facts and norms* Habermas (1996) would differentiate this conception by placing the political public sphere in the periphery of the political system and thus between the lifeworld and the center of the political system. But the normative demand that communication in the public sphere should be rooted in and informed by the interactions in the lifeworld remains a central tenet of Habermas's approach.

Analyzing the lifeworld is only one perspective in Habermas's theory of society. As we have seen, the other perspective focuses on the *systems of administrative power* and *of the economy*. Systems can be analyzed without a participant's perspective. Their functional imperatives and effects are identified best from a non-participant observer's point of view. Politics allocates decision-making powers and produces collectively binding decisions; the economy allocates resources and produces wealth distributions. Habermas is not concerned about the regular functioning of these systems. In fact, in his view they perform exclusive functions that cannot be performed by other systems or by the lifeworld and that are necessary for the existence of highly differentiated modern societies.

What Habermas is concerned about is the disturbances that the two systems create in the lifeworld when their imperatives supersede the communicative logic of interaction there – a process he calls "colonization" of the lifeworld. In table 2.2 we have already encountered the crisis symptoms that this kind of colonization creates for the three structural components of the lifeworld. Habermas summarizes them as follows: In cultural reproduction, systemic imperatives destroy the intersubjectively produced meanings and traditions and therefore produce a cultural impoverishment ("loss of meaning") that dries up the basis for mutual understanding. In social integration, the colonizing impulse creates anomie, in which legitimately ordered relations of solidarity are dissolved and people feel alienated from their fellow citizens. And in socialization, identity formation is disrupted and mental illnesses result from the intrusion of purely functional logics into the relations that people establish with themselves. Compared to the earlier incarnation of the colonization thesis in *Structural transformation of the public sphere*, the critical diagnosis encapsulated in it has become much more precise and differentiated in *The theory of communicative action*. But the normative content of that critique remains largely the same.

If we translate the colonization diagnosis to the functioning of public spheres, it becomes clear that for Habermas both cultural production and political will-formation must be kept as free of the imperatives of power and money as possible. Habermas therefore fiercely opposes a commercialization of science, art, the media, and education as well as a submergence of political communication and free will-formation under the power of governmental and other political strategists. This normative stance subsequently leads him to develop a conception of media and democracy in which discursive will-formation is central (see chapter 3).

As we have seen, Habermas locates these discursive processes of political will-formation in the lifeworld, more precisely in the domain of social integration in which group-based relations of solidarity are produced. At the same time, he also identifies politics as one of the two systems exclusively regulated by their own norm-free functional imperatives of power distribution, which threaten to colonize the lifeworld. This is no contradiction. The tension that seems to exist here is due to the tension between two sub-domains of the political system associated with communicative power on the one hand and administrative power on the other. Politics is both a process of discussion and learning oriented to the common good, which produces *communicative power*, and a process of interest coordination in which the social power of societal actors is converted into administrative power, which is then used to implement decisions. Learning takes place in the periphery and decisions are taken in the center of the political system.

SUMMARY

In Habermas's oeuvre, *The theory of communicative action* stands between his early work on the *Structural transformation of the public sphere* and his later conception of deliberative democracy in *Between facts and norms*. The *Theory of communicative action* preserves the early normative impulses: a concern for rational-critical exchanges in the public sphere and a critique of the colonization of everyday communication by money and power. In doing so, it provides a new micro foundation for rationality and a clearer conception of the colonization of the lifeworld.

The new foundation for rational-critical exchange lies in the concept of "communication oriented to reaching understanding" as the quintessential form of communication in which we all inadvertently make three counterfactual presuppositions, namely that truth, moral rightness, and truthfulness are realized in individual communicative acts. Rational-critical discourse is then understood as discourse that problematizes either truth claims (in theoretical discourse) or validity claims to moral rightness (in practical discourse). These two types of discourses correspond to two of the three structural components of the lifeworld, namely "culture" and "society," and are thus deeply ingrained in our lifeworld. The problematization of truth claims contributes to the reproduction and innovation of the cultural knowledge base from which we draw to make sense of the world, whereas the problematization of rightness claims contributes to the reproduction and innovation of legitimate social relations from which we develop solidarity with others. Both types of discourses have institutionalized homes in larger specialized action systems: science, religion, and art for knowledge reproduction, and politics and law for legitimate social orders.

But the crucial point for Habermas's theorization of media and public debate lies in the fact that both forms of discourse find fertile breeding grounds in specialized communicative spaces and particular media environments: Knowledge and truth claims are circulated and discussed in the cultural public sphere grounded in specialized magazines or quality newspapers, as well as in more general forums of cultural reflection both on- and offline. The legitimacy of social relations and the societal order, on the other hand, is discussed in the political public sphere, which finds its home in the news media as well as offline and online discussion and mobilization. In the real world the cultural and the political public spheres are not as separate as they might appear in this theoretical conceptualization. In the less specialized and more popular media forums both types of discourses are often intertwined. But note that the distinction relates back to Habermas's early analysis of the literary public sphere in eighteenth-century Europe that only later turned more political and contestatory vis-à-vis the state (see chapter 1).

Finally, despite the full-fledged model of three types of validity claims and three components of the lifeworld in the *Theory of communicative action*, Habermas is actually most interested in its "middle part": validity claims to moral rightness, practical discourse about legitimate social relations, the political public sphere as its breeding ground, and politics and law as the two systems that specialize in regulating the social order. It is no wonder, therefore, that the third major book, *Between facts and norms*, to which we turn in the following chapter, is largely a theory of law and politics, which features the political public sphere as a vital component that ensures the rooting of law and politics in the discourses of the lifeworld. Habermas's comprehensive conception of the lifeworld, however, was and still is largely lost in discussions of his work in media and communication studies. This is due in part to the fact that the theory was published in English (in 1984 and 1987) *before* the English translation of the *Structural transformation of the public sphere* finally came out, in 1989, and made Habermas a household name among Anglophone communication scholars. In discussing *Structural transformation* in the early 1990s few communication scholars actually went "back," as it were, to the *Theory of communicative action*, which at the time already provided a highly sophisticated differentiation and extension of Habermas's original account, which would have helped to put the much-criticized early idealization of the bourgeois public sphere in perspective. There remains much to be discovered for students of media and communication in Habermas's distinctions between different types of validity claims and problematizing discourses. This includes, as we will see in chapter 7, a nascent conception of the role of emotions in mediated public discussion that builds on his concept of practical discourse – something that very few people would ever have associated with Habermas's name.

RECOMMENDED READING

Honneth, A. and Joas, H. (eds.) (1991) *Communicative action: Essays on Jürgen Habermas's The Theory of Communicative Action.* MIT Press, Boston, MA. (This includes Habermas's own rejoinder to his critics.)

3

MEDIA FOR DELIBERATIVE
DEMOCRACY

How exactly are concerns and discussions from the lifeworld channeled and infused into decision-making at the center of the political system? And what is the role of the media in this process? These are the questions that Habermas treats in chapter 8 of his book *Between facts and norms* (1996). The basic assumptions remain those that we already know from his *Theory of communicative action*, but Habermas describes the intermediation between lifeworld and political decision-making in much greater detail here and by using a much wider array of literature than before. One particular point of inspiration for Habermas is the work of his student and later colleague Bernhard Peters (1949–2005). It took the help of Peters's model for Habermas to develop a clearer grasp of the structures and processes of the political public sphere, which he had endeavored to dissect since his early book on the *Structural transformation of the public sphere*.

THE POLITICAL PUBLIC SPHERE IN ACTION

Habermas adopts three theoretical elements from Peters (1993). First, the political system is conceived along a *center–periphery* axis. The center is made up of a polyarchic structure that comprises the administration/government, the judicial system, and democratic opinion- and will-formation in parliaments, elections, and party competition (Habermas 1996, 354f.). The periphery branches out into an input and output periphery. On the output side, private organizations like business associations, labor unions, and other interest groups fulfill certain coordination tasks in implementing the decisions made in the center. On the input side, a slew of different actors attempt to insert societal concerns into the parliamentary and the judicial sectors. These range from clearly particularistic organizations interested only in their own benefit all the way to public-interest groups representing weakly organized interests and common goods.

Second, the center area of the political system is organized as a system of *sluices*, democratic and constitutional procedures through which concerns and demands must be channeled in order to affect political decision-making. This ensemble of procedures acting as sluices to societal demands "is the only way to exclude the possibility that the power of the administrative complex, on the one side, or the social power of the intermediate structures affecting the core area, on the other side, become independent vis-à-vis a communicative power that develops in the parliamentary complex" (Habermas 1996, 356). In other words, the sluices make sure that power-holders in society and politics cannot directly impose their will, but are reined in via democratic procedures.

Third, Peters (1993, 346) and subsequently Habermas (1996, 357) distinguish a *routine mode and a crisis mode of problem-solving.* The "official" circulation of power – from the periphery through parliaments (or courts) and government decisions to the implementation by the administration – is only realized when the autonomous public spheres in the periphery problematize a particular issue and public opinion builds enough pressure to entice core institutions to follow their constitutionally prescribed roles. On the other hand, in the intermediary periods between such peaks of problematization, the flow of communication and decision is often top-down, starting in government agencies and trickling down to the periphery without much resistance. Habermas sees this as normatively unproblematic as long as the routine mode does not favor particularistic interests in extreme ways and as long as the center can be forced to return to the crisis mode by periphery mobilization at any time.

With these three basic assumptions in hand Habermas (1996, 359–87) proceeds to describe in detail what happens in the political public sphere. The political public sphere reflexively stabilizes itself through the utterances of its participants.

> Actors who know they are involved in the *common* enterprise of reconstituting and maintaining structures of the public sphere as they contest opinions and strive for influence differ from actors who merely use forums that already exist. More specifically, actors who support the public sphere are distinguished by the *dual orientation* of their political engagement: with their programs, they directly influence the political system, but at the same time they are also reflexively concerned with revitalizing and enlarging civil society and the public sphere as well as with confirming their own identities and capacities to act. (Habermas 1996, 369f.)

The relationship between the sphere of public contention rooted in civil society and the decision-making core of the political system is characterized by a certain type of restraint. Public discourses cannot transform society on the whole or act on its behalf. "To generate political power, their influence must have an effect on the democratically elected assemblies and assume an authorized form in formal decisions" (Habermas 1996, 372), and this effect can in no way be taken for granted. Internally, the public sphere is not a monolithic block. Instead, it

represents a highly complex network that branches out into a multitude of overlapping international, national, regional, local, and subcultural arenas. Functional specifications, thematic foci, policy fields, and so forth, provide the points of reference for a substantive differentiation of public spheres that are, however, still accessible to laypersons (for example, popular science and literary publics, religious and artistic publics, feminist and "alternative" publics, publics concerned with healthcare issues, social welfare, or environmental policy). Moreover, the public sphere is differentiated into levels according to the density of communication, organizational complexity, and range – from the *episodic* publics found in taverns, coffee houses, or on the streets; through the *occasional* or "arranged" publics of particular presentations and events, such as theater performances, rock concerts, party assemblies, or church congresses; up to the *abstract* public sphere of isolated readers, listeners, and viewers scattered across large geographic areas, or even around the globe, and brought together only through the mass media. (Habermas 1996, 373f.)

Habermas's point with respect to this cacophony of arenas, groups, sites, and occasions is not differentiation or segmentation *per se*, but the fact "that all the partial publics constituted by ordinary language remain porous to one another" and that every exclusion mechanism can always be taken back (Habermas 1996, 374). "The public sphere" still exists as one because what is being said in one segment remains translatable to what occupies another, and vice versa. The sphere of public expression and contention does not fall entirely apart precisely because it is rooted in communication that is in principle understandable to everybody.

MEDIA POWER

The public sphere is populated by different types of actors. Habermas distinguishes "authochtone" actors who genuinely emerge from the public from those actors who use the existing structures of public communication and merely appear before the public (Habermas 1996, 375). This distinction is reminiscent of Habermas's (1989b) earlier juxtaposition of "critical publicity" and "representative publicness" (see chapter 1). In addition, journalists and other media personnel acquire a distinct form of power, the "power of the media," by virtue of their gatekeeping role and presentation choices (Habermas 1996, 376). In Habermas's view this power is not used to benefit democracy, at least not by the electronic media. "Reporting facts as human-interest stories, mixing information with entertainment, arranging material episodically, and breaking down complex relationships into smaller fragments – all of this comes together to form a syndrome that works to depoliticize public communication. This is the kernel of truth in the theory of the culture industry" (Habermas 1996, 377). Thirty-five years after his *Structural transformation of the public sphere* Habermas has recourse here again to the older tradition of critical theory, with its emphasis on the counter-enlightening tendencies of the culture industry, even though his *Theory of communicative action* had endeavored to supersede that tradition with a new theoretical foundation based on the concept of communicative action (see Benson 2009, 182). This is all the more astonishing as Habermas at the same time acknowledges the latitude that active audiences possess in interpreting media content in subversive ways. He also concedes that "it is by no means clear how the mass media intervene in the diffuse circuits of communication in the political public sphere" (Habermas 1996, 377). More than a decade after *Between facts and norms* Habermas will return to this point and develop a more precise model of this intervention of the mass media in political communication processes in his essay "Political communication in media society" (Habermas 2009b). For the time being, however, he refrains from pursuing this empirical question further, and turns instead to the normative foundations of a democratic media system, which by recourse to Gurevitch and Blumler (1990) he summarizes in the following terms:

> [T]he mass media ought to understand themselves as the mandatary of an enlightened public whose willingness to learn and capacity for criticism they at once presuppose, demand, and reinforce; like the judiciary, they ought to preserve their independence from political and social pressure; they ought to be receptive to the public's concerns and proposals, take up these issues and contributions impartially, augment criticisms, and confront the political process with articulate demands for legitimation. (Habermas 1996, 378)

Whereas the prospects for civil society's influence on the political process are judged to be quite bleak in the routine phases, the power balance is shifted in favor of civil society in crisis situations. During such periods new problems and grievances are articulated by

> intellectuals, concerned citizens, radical professionals, self-proclaimed "advocates," and the like. Moving in from this outermost periphery, such issues force their way into newspapers and interested associations, clubs, professional organizations, academies, and universities. They find forums, citizen initiatives, and other platforms before they catalyze the growth of social movements and new subcultures. The latter can in turn dramatize contributions, presenting them so effectively that the mass media take up the matter. Only through their controversial presentation in the media do such topics reach the larger public and subsequently gain a place on the "public agenda." Sometimes the support of sensational actions, mass protests, and incessant campaigning is required before an issue can make its way via the surprising election of marginal candidates or radical parties, expanded platforms of "established" parties, important court decisions, and so on, into the core of the political system and there receive formal consideration. (Habermas 1996, 381)

In contrast to widespread beliefs among his critics, Habermas paints a positive picture here of robust, uncivil forms of bottom-up campaigning – if they serve to "besiege" the core of the political system rather than denigrate and vilify other actors. Habermas's approval extends even further: "The last means for obtaining more of a hearing and greater media influence for oppositional arguments are acts of civil disobedience. These acts of nonviolent, symbolic rule violation are meant as expressions of protest against binding decisions that, their legality notwithstanding, the actors consider illegitimate in the light of valid constitutional principles"

(Habermas 1996, 382f.). We should keep this in mind when we turn to the role of counterpublics and emotions in chapter 7.

DEEP MEDIA DEMOCRACY

Habermas's (as yet) most recent contribution to media theory is his essay "Political communication in media society: Does democracy still have an epistemic dimension? The impact of normative theory on empirical research" (Habermas 2009b). This essay can in many ways be read as his legacy in theorizing deliberation and the media and it is, fittingly, dedicated to his late colleague Bernhard Peters, who, as we have seen, had already inspired Habermas's thinking on the media in *Between facts and norms*. In summarizing this legacy, Habermas offers, for the first time, a visual depiction of the political communication process as he envisions it (see figures 3.1 and 3.2).

In the first part of the essay, Habermas places the media at the center of democracy. All democracies share three characteristics: they guarantee the legal protection of the private sphere, the political participation of as many interested citizens as possible, and the "appropriate contribution of a public sphere to the formation of considered public opinions" (Habermas 2009b, 141). This contribution is secured through three design elements of democratic systems:

- a separation between the tax-gathering state and a market-based society [...];
- freedom of the press, diversity of the mass media, and freedom of information; and
- regulations guaranteeing mass audiences and civil society access to the public sphere and preventing the monopolization of arenas of public communication by political, social, or economic interests. (p. 141)

This is a strong statement couched in unobtrusive terms. It is not enough that the media are able to report freely (and thus also to criticize government), but they should also be diverse, enjoy privileged access to official documents ("freedom of information"), be accessible to citizens who want to speak up, and at the same time be insulated from the influence of various power-holders in society including government agencies and corporations. I will call this conception *deep media democracy*.

Deep media democracy is both a fundamental theoretical tool and a rhetorical instrument with which the public intellectual Jürgen Habermas criticizes time and again what he sees as aberrations in the media industry. No wonder then that Habermas, later in his 2009 essay, scathingly dismisses the concentration of economic and political power personified in the 2000s by media moguls such as Silvio Berlusconi and Rupert Murdoch. No wonder also that Habermas is deeply alarmed by the takeover of leading quality media (such as his favorite daily, *Süddeutsche Zeitung*, in Germany) by financial investment firms that have much higher profit expectations than the traditional, culturally entrenched family owners. In his intervention "Media, markets and consumers: The quality press as the backbone of the political public sphere" (2009a) he therefore advocates for creative forms of subsidy and public finance for quality media in order to ensure deep media democracy. This may be due to the influence of C. Edwin Baker's (2002) analysis of market failure in the media realm and the responsibility of the state to counter it (see Benson 2009, 191).

For Habermas, deep media democracy is so important because it constitutes the breeding ground in which mediated macro deliberation can flourish:

> The deliberative model conceives of the public sphere as a sounding board for registering problems which affect society as a whole, and at the same time as a discursive filter-bed

which sifts interest-generalizing and informative contributions to relevant topics out of the unregulated processes of opinion formation, broadcasts these "public opinions" back onto the dispersed public of citizens, and puts them on the formal agendas of the responsible bodies. (Habermas 2009b, 143)

The public sphere as a sounding board and filter bed will then exert a "rationalizing pressure toward improving the *quality* of decisions" (p. 143).

MEDIA FUNCTIONS IN THE DELIBERATIVE SYSTEM

But how exactly is this process of rationalization through public debate supposed to work? Before Habermas goes on to spell out the elements and processes of macro deliberation in deep media democracy he first makes a strategic qualification. "[T]he rationalizing power of the political public sphere should extend only to the formation of opinions, not to political decisions" (Habermas 2009b, 146). The latter should be rationalized by formal deliberation in courts, parliaments, cabinet meetings, etc. With this argument Habermas both responds and contributes to the recent systemic turn in deliberative theory introduced by Parkinson and Mansbridge (2012). Each deliberative forum and political institution performs a different function in and for the overall deliberative system.

The juxtaposition of formalized micro deliberation and unregulated mediated macro deliberation then leads Habermas (2009b) to forgo all deliberative demands directly addressed to the mass media.

The kind of media-based mass communication with which we are familiar from national public spheres is not subject to any standard of discursive quality, or even representativeness. In virtue of its structure alone, it lacks certain characteristic features of a discursive dispute. In comparison to institutionalized opinion and will formation, two deficits in particular stand out: The lack of straightforward, face-to-face interactions, between really (or virtually) present participants, in a shared practice of collective decision-making; and the lack of reciprocity between the roles of speakers and addressees in an egalitarian exchange of opinions and claims. (Habermas 2009b, 154)

In addition, mass communication is in Habermas's perspective deeply imbued with social power – the power of the media to select and present at their will and the historically variable power of political and economic power-holders to influence media content. Such power, as we have seen, runs counter to the idea of deep media democracy.

In Habermas's view, thus, mass communication with its one-to-many structure of message distribution cannot be expected to generate discursive exchanges and rational outcomes because readers and viewers are not compelled to immediately react and speakers are thus not directly challenged. The central actors on the stage of the political public sphere – journalists and politicians – are not interested in convincing each other, but "try to shape the opinions of an anonymous public without having to expose themselves to critical questioning" (Habermas 2009b, 157). (In chapter 5 we will see how, despite this claim, communication scholars have used the deliberative framework to exactly measure the deliberativeness of political media content and how that serves to further develop deliberative media theory in ways that Habermas has not foreseen.)

Is the Internet the solution to this problem? Not so, in Habermas's view. Under liberal regimes

> the emergence of millions of "chat rooms" scattered throughout the world and of globally networked "issue publics" tends rather to fragment the huge mass public, which in the public sphere is centered on the same issues at the same time in spite of its size. This public disintegrates in virtual space into a large number of contingent fragmented groups, held together by special interests. [...] For the present, there are no functional equivalents, in this virtual space, for the structures of publicity which reassemble the decentralized messages, sift them, and synthesize them in edited form. [...] Political communication within national publics seems at present to be able to benefit from online debates only when groups which are active on the Web refer to real processes, such as election campaigns or current controversies, for example, in an attempt to mobilize the interest and support of members. (Habermas 2009b, 157f.)

Thus, Habermas places no hope for macro deliberation in freewheeling online discourse and is prepared to grant democratic benefits only to organization-bound mobilization.

Habermas finds the solution to the simultaneous problems of asymmetrical and power-imbued mass communication and fragmented Internet discourse in the division of labor between different modes and arenas of communication (see figure 3.1). Media-based mass communication is freed from immediate deliberative demands and placed at the center of the political public sphere. "The public sphere forms the loosely structured periphery to the densely populated institutional centre of the state, and it is rooted in turn in the still more fleeting communicative networks of civil society"

Modes of communication	Arenas of political communication	
Institutionalized discourses and negotiations	Government, administration, parliaments, courts, etc.	Political system (1) State institutions
Media-based mass communications in dispersed public spheres	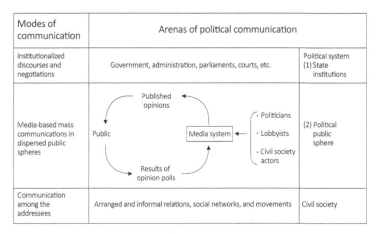	(2) Political public sphere
Communication among the addressees	Arranged and informal relations, social networks, and movements	Civil society

Figure 3.1 Arenas of political communication, as conceived by Habermas (adapted from Habermas 2009b, 160)

(Habermas 2009b, 159). Internet discourse is positioned on the level of "communication among the addressees." Habermas sees empirical evidence for the rationalizing effect of deliberation both on the upper level of institutionalized political discourse and negotiations and on the lower level of everyday citizen conversation. On the intermediate level of mediated political communication, the media system produces published opinions that are selected from the supply of opinions offered by politicians, lobbyists, and pressure groups as well as civil society actors and experts. Published opinions are absorbed by the dispersed public and fed back into the media system as aggregated individual preferences in the form of opinion polls.

CONSIDERED PUBLIC OPINIONS

In order to evaluate the potential benefits of this inner circuit of mediated political communication Habermas further specifies its central output, i.e. public opinions, and observes

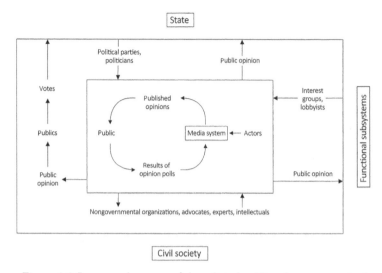

Figure 3.2 Inputs and outputs of the political public sphere, as conceived by Habermas (adapted from Habermas 2009b, 166)

how these are processed outside the media system, in the wider field of societal communication (figure 3.2). Public opinions are

> clusters of controversial issues and inputs to which the parties concerned intuitively attach *weights* in accordance with their perceptions of the cumulative "yes" and "no" stances of the wider public. Public opinions exert influence. They form a milieu to which thoughts and feelings adjust, and thereby they exercise an indirect pressure on opinions and attitudes; in the long run, they influence the formation of mentalities. (Habermas 2009b, 165)

Public opinions are not identical to the opinions published by the media, or to the empirical opinions of the individual citizens. Instead they are outcomes of an "intuitive bridging" of both, "the efforts of opinion-forming elites and of the more or less conscious reactions of a broad and diverse mass audience" (p. 165).

Habermas is not specific about how this "bridging" might actually work, but it is clear that public opinions are the products of multi-sited, collective *perceptions* of both published opinions and aggregated mass opinions. For Habermas's evaluative purposes it is more important to see what happens next: Public opinions are not the final product but are themselves subjected to additional rounds of reflection on both the upper and lower decks of political communication. "People can take *an additional* stance on what they perceive as public opinion. Such reflexive responses 'from above', from the political system, and 'from below', from civil society, constitute a double test of how effectively political communication functions as a filtering mechanism" (Habermas 2009b, 166). If mediated political communication filters opinions competently, the result of this additional reflection will be "considered public opinions." "By this term I understand a pair of contrary, more or less coherent opinions, weighted in accordance with agreement and disagreement, which refer to a relevant issue and express what appears at the time, in the light of available information, to be the most plausible or reasoned interpretations of a sufficiently relevant – though generally controversial – issue" (p. 166).

SUMMARY

In Habermas's view mediated political communication is not itself deliberative, nor should it be expected to be deliberative. But it can under favorable conditions produce beneficial outcomes – namely, considered public opinions – and "thus it can contribute to the deliberative quality of the political process in the way envisaged for this sector by the deliberative model" (Habermas 2009b, 167). Mediated political communication is supposed to fulfill only the first function of deliberation, namely "that relevant issues and controversial answers, requisite information and appropriate arguments for and against will be mobilized" (Habermas 2009b, 162).

The two additional functions are reserved for other arenas of communication and decision: "that the alternatives which emerge will be subjected to examination in argumentation and will be evaluated accordingly; and that rationally motivated 'yes' and 'no' positions on procedurally correct decisions will be the deciding factor" in political decision-making (p. 162). In Habermas's view the media are sounding boards and filter beds, but not "argumentation arenas." They support deliberation that then takes place in parliaments, courts, and cabinets.

It stands to reason that Habermas would not mind deliberative media content at all, even though he does not want to normatively overburden the media. But it remains curious that he searches for conducive and detrimental conditions of deliberation in citizens' motivations and competencies as well as in the legal regulations of the media system, but not in the actual professional performance of media practitioners and its variance across media types and media systems. It is the purpose of chapter 5 to show how Habermas's conception of deliberation has been fruitfully employed to do exactly this – and to highlight those factors that drive deliberative media performance.

But there is a deeper point here, too. As shown in figures 3.1 and 3.2, Habermas assigns the media very clear, but strictly circumscribed functional roles in the process of political opinion- and will-formation. In doing so, he deemphasizes other, broader roles that mediated communication can play in society. Mediated public debates create collective self-understandings and help enact collective identities, which reach beyond discussing political yes-and-no questions. Mediated public spheres are culture-producing sites in addition to policy-legitimizing venues. In fact, it is a strength of the deliberative perspective that it conceives democracy not only as a decision-producing mechanism but essentially as a large-scale experiment in collective learning. As Bernhard Peters (2008c, 237) has so aptly put it:

> The "opinion-formation model" of public deliberation is certainly correct. It specifies essential functions that public deliberation should provide in a democracy. But as such, it only gives *a severely truncated version of what public deliberation is or should be about*. Public deliberation is not just about people making up their minds on topics that are on the public agenda, using available information and opinions. Public deliberation should be much more. [...] It should be about the *identification* of problems and about a *collective search for new solutions*. It should not just be about the resolution of immediate political questions. It should also involve a more general debate about worldviews, values and principles and collective self-understandings. It is about collective solutions, but it is also about *intellectual and cultural innovation* and producing and distributing new ideas and interpretations. (Peters 2008c, 237; italics in the original)

To gauge this cultural innovation function of the media in a deliberative democracy it is necessary to revive Habermas's older ideas about the cultural public sphere and look for the contribution that non-deliberative media forms can make to genuine public debate in a deliberative democracy (see chapter 6). Before we turn to such questions, however, it is necessary to demarcate this learning-oriented, deliberative understanding of democracy from its main normative rivals, which is the topic of the next chapter.

RECOMMENDED READING

Benson, R. (2009) "Shaping the public sphere: Habermas and beyond," *The American Sociologist*, 40, pp. 175–92. doi: 10.1007/s12108-009-9071-4.

Parkinson, J. and Mansbridge, J. (eds.) (2012) *Deliberative systems: Deliberative democracy at the large scale*. Cambridge University Press, Cambridge.

Peters, B. (2008c) "Public discourse, identity and the problem of democratic legitimacy." In: Wessler, H. (ed.) *Public deliberation and public culture: The writings of Bernhard Peters, 1993–2005*. Palgrave Macmillan, London, pp. 213–54.

4

MEDIATED PUBLIC SPHERES

For the purposes of this book, normative models of democracy are primarily interesting because they support different normative expectations vis-à-vis the media and the functioning of mediated public spheres. The following contrast of normative models is therefore geared toward distilling "purified" types that can guide empirical analysis, even if this means that my account cannot do justice to all the philosophical underpinnings and ramifications of each tradition. I will contrast Habermas's deliberative model of democracy and political communication with its main rivals, the liberal, the republican, and the agonistic models.

In looking at the different models I will identify one central value that the respective model prioritizes at the expense of other values, as well as one central metaphor that captures the model's view of the mediated public sphere (table 4.1). I then specify what each model has to say about the desired input of mediated public debates ("Who should talk?"), their throughput ("How should these actors speak?"),

Table 4.1 Normative expectations vis-à-vis mediated public spheres

	Central value	Central metaphor for the public sphere	Input: Who should talk?	Throughput: How should they talk?	Outcome: Under what conditions should public debate stop?
Liberal model	Freedom	Mirror of society	Representation model: representatives from societal groups (proportional)	Various communication styles are accepted (if adequate level of respect is given)	Closure of debate after majority opinion has emerged
Republican model	Community	Amicable conversation	Community model: those sharing basic values or beliefs	Internal dialogue, justification, respect, and civility	Closure of debate after shared values and mutual commitments have been reaffirmed
Deliberative model	Public reasons	Discussion group	Participation model: inclusion of all those affected by the issue	External dialogue, justification, respect, and civility	Closure of debate through argumentatively supported majority opinion (reasoned dissent)
Agonistic model	Difference	Protest march	Empowerment model: popular inclusion with particular emphasis on marginalized groups	Narration, expressive self-presentation, rhetoric	Avoid closure, keep opportunities for autonomous articulation open in pursuit of a new counter-hegemonic order

and their outcome ("Under what conditions should public debate stop?"). This threefold distinction is based on similar accounts in Ferree et al. (2002, 229), Peters (2008d, 122), Gerhards, Neidhardt, and Rucht (1998, 37), Baker (2002), Benson (2009), Strömbäck (2005), Freelon (2015), Dahlberg (2001; 2011), and Wessler and Rinke (2012). Each of these accounts gives a somewhat different structure to the field of media-related models of democracy, sometimes mixing models that other authors have separated and sometimes introducing additional models for the purpose of making a specific point. But most of them are compatible with the distinctions I will make in the following.

We will begin by looking at Habermas's own view of the field of democratic theory. In justifying his deliberative conception of democracy, Habermas (1994) distinguishes it from the liberal and the republican traditions in democratic theory.

> The institutional design of modern democracies combines three elements: the private autonomy of citizens, each one of whom has the right to pursue a life of her own; democratic citizenship, that is, the uniform inclusion of free and equal citizens in the political community; and an independent public sphere, which functions as an intermediary domain between state and society and in which citizens form opinions and desires. [...] Although these three elements – equal liberties, democratic participation, and government by public opinion – are fused into a single design within the family of constitutional states, they are accorded different relative weights in different traditions. The liberal tradition reveals a preference for the liberties of private citizens, whereas the republican and the deliberative traditions stress the political participation of active citizens in the democratic process and in the formation of considered public opinions, respectively. (Habermas 2009b, 139–41)

THE LIBERAL MODEL

In the liberal model of democracy (see table 4.1, first row), citizens are seen as pursuing their private, pre-political interests and expressing their preferences primarily through elections. Freedom primarily entails the freedom from state intervention in private affairs. When citizens organize to further their private interests, an "interest-group democracy" (Baker 2002, 135) emerges. The public sphere serves to make the interests and opinions of these groups transparent by giving voice to their representatives. In public discourse, groups are prioritized in accordance with their relative strength in the real world. The media are supposed to provide a mirror image of society in which citizens can observe their own representatives and those of other groups and gain an overview of the respective opinions and preferences. Provided that a basic level of respect is maintained, no specific demands are directed at how the debate should be conducted; non-dialogic communication styles such as mere pronouncements or robust advocacy are perfectly acceptable (Neidhardt 1994, 20). Given the media's limited carrying capacity and citizens' limited attention span, debates should terminate when positions are clarified and a majority opinion has crystallized, to make room for other important issues (Ferree et al. 2002, 210).

Habermas criticizes this conception of democracy as instrumentalist and sharply juxtaposes it with "the republican ethics of citizenship, in which the pathos of national self-determination finds expression" (Habermas 2009b, 142). "Here [in republicanism] the construction of the constitutional state is conceived in terms of the goal of facilitating a practice of self-determination which is conducted jointly by the united citizenry and not, as in the liberal tradition, with a view to facilitating each individual's autonomous conduct of life" (Habermas 2009b, 142). Similarly, Baker points out that

> [i]nterest-group pluralism neglects two basic attributes of most people and these attributes are central to a sounder democratic theory. First, people are not, certainly not always, narrowly self-interested. People are social, communal, and often caring and idealistic, not purely selfish and atomistic. [...] People are often motivated by conceptions of a common good and by a concern with others' welfare. Second, people's interests do not spring full blown from some inner source or even from their group identity. Rather, people expend considerable effort in formulating, evaluating, and choosing interests and values to which they then give allegiance. (Baker 2002, 138f.)

These criticisms of the liberal model are addressed in the second, republican tradition of democratic theory (table 4.1, second row).

THE REPUBLICAN MODEL

In the republican tradition, citizens are seen as members of a political community engaged in amicable conversation about what is best for them. Media are supposed to facilitate that conversation by offering platforms, online and offline, in which people who share basic values and beliefs can exchange ideas and self-identify as a community. The conversation should be respectful and civil, with members justifying their positions and actively seeking the common good and a collective self-understanding with fellow members. However, "[c]ommunity members in this sense tend to be strongly interested in advancing community prerogatives and relatively uninterested in engaging cooperatively with non-members" (Freelon 2015, 775). Thus, debates should close once the shared values and mutual commitments among community members have been publicly reaffirmed. To this end, argumentative and celebratory elements in public discourse can intertwine.

Habermas is sympathetic to the republican model's emphasis on the active participation of citizens in determining the common good. At the same time he is critical of two other aspects of the model that devalue this participatory premise. For Habermas the republican model is, first, too idealistic and, second, too closely tied to the maintenance of concrete communities (Habermas 1994, 4f.). What does this mean? In the republican model "democracy is dependent on the virtue of citizens devoted to the public weal. This expectation of virtue already led Rousseau to split the citizen oriented to the common good from the private man, who cannot be ethically overburdened. The unanimity of the political legislature was supposed to be secured in advance by a substantive ethical consensus" (Habermas 1994, 4). "Ethical consensus" here means that citizens agree in their conceptions of the good life and of the society they want to live in. Thus, in Habermas's view, the republican model demands too much public-spiritedness from the individual and must therefore presuppose a substantive consensus between citizens on the ethical foundations of their living together. An ethical consensus, however, always refers to a concrete community of real people and thus ties democracy to their collective self-understanding.

To be sure, discourses aimed at achieving self-understanding – discourses in which the participants want to get a clear understanding of themselves as members of a specific nation, as members of a locale or a state, as inhabitants of a region, etc.; in which they want to determine which traditions they will continue; in which they strive to determine how they will treat each other, and how they will treat minorities and marginal groups; in short, discourses in which they want to get clear about the kind of society they want to live in – such discourses are also an important part of politics. But these questions are subordinate to moral questions and connected with pragmatic questions. (Habermas 1994, 4f.)

Moral questions are questions of justice, i.e. considerations about "how a matter can be regulated in the equal interest of all" (Habermas 1994, 5) even if ethical self-understandings between groups of citizens diverge or contradict each other, as they mostly do in modern pluralistic societies. And pragmatic questions are about how such regulations can be implemented most effectively. According to Habermas, the task of democratic politics is not primarily to uphold a foundation of common values in a political community, but to find creative and workable ways in which justice can be approximated when citizens adhere to opposing values. And for such a task, Habermas contends, democracy requires a type of mediated discourse quite different from the republican brand of amicable conversation between people sharing values.

THE DELIBERATIVE MODEL

In Habermas's deliberative model of democracy, public communication resembles a discussion group writ large (see table 4.1, third row). In a deliberative democracy, communicative engagements are marked by disagreement but at the same time propelled by participants advancing public reasons for their diverging positions. Public debate should include all those affected by the issue discussed, or at least the perspectives and experiences of all those affected and the reasons that support their views (Wessler 2008). In order for such reasons to gain legitimacy they must be weighed against the justifications that other, opposing actors advance for their own views. Such exchange of reasons should span the lines of difference rather than remain within one group. It should also happen in a climate of mutual respect and civility. In mediated public communication it is unlikely that a substantive consensus will be achieved across lines of difference even if moral rather than ethical consensus is expected. Therefore, the desired outcome of communicative engagements in the public sphere lies in argumentatively supported majority opinions or, more generally, reasoned dissent (Wessler 2008). Debate should not close before this epistemic gain of public exchange has been realized, i.e. before participants have a clearer idea about why they adhere to their positions and what the reasons are that others advance for their alternative positions. The deliberative model advances a procedural understanding of public communication: The desirable democratic benefits are created in the process of deliberative discussion itself, rather than through an ethical consensus (that is impossible to achieve in pluralistic societies) like the republican model would have it, or a mere aggregation of self-interested opinions like in the liberal model.

However, the deliberative model of mediated communication has been subjected to a number of criticisms that are relevant here.[1] Mouffe (1999) and Sanders (1997, 348f.) argue that the deliberative demand for civil speech and the focus on fact-based argumentation systematically favors some groups over others (see also Dahlberg 2014). According to these critics, this contradicts the deliberative claim for broad inclusion of everybody affected by an issue in the discussion and neglects the putative benefits of passions and emotions for democratic discourse (Mouffe 1999, 755f.). These criticisms gave rise to a fourth normative model of mediated public spheres.

THE AGONISTIC MODEL

The word "agonistic" derives from the ancient Greek word *agon*, which means quarrel, dispute, fight. The agonistic model thus favors robust value exchanges that highlight difference, mostly associated with radical politics. The model of public communication enshrined in this view most resembles a vigorous, colorful protest march that empowers formerly marginalized groups and helps them find ways of authentic self-expression. The forms of expression favored in agonistic theory eschew argumentation and focus on narrative, rhetoric, and expressive self-presentation (Ferree et al. 2002, 226; Young 1996). Because opportunities for such self-expression are seen as rare and curtailed in a given hegemonic order, most agonists aim at avoiding closure of debate. Instead they want to keep channels for autonomous articulation open at all times, especially for marginalized groups.

More recently, agonists have discussed the necessity of developing a positive alternative political order as part of the agonistic project (see Glover 2012, 91): "I do not think that one can envisage the nature of the agonistic struggle simply in terms of an ongoing contestation over issues or identities. One also needs to grasp the crucial role of hegemonic articulations and the necessity not only of challenging what exists but also of constructing new articulations and new institutions" (Mouffe 2013, 11). But such new articulations and institutions are constructed in order not to end public debate but to forge a more forceful, unified coalition of allies to engage in public contestation (see table 4.1, fourth row). Mouffe (2013, 7) maintains that any political struggle creates a confrontation between "us" and "them" because it is unavoidably built on antagonistic interests that cannot be reconciled at all, let alone through public debate. According to the agonistic model, public discourse is thus always imbued with power and a struggle for hegemony, albeit fought between adversaries, not enemies (p. 7).

How, then, does the agonistic model relate to Habermas's deliberative conception? While the agonistic criticism raises important issues, some of its representatives fail to recognize changes within the deliberative framework which take up and respond to this criticism. For example, Young (1996) agrees with the agonistic critics that the criteria of moderate and civil speech negatively affect the claim for broad inclusion because they discriminate against speech by underprivileged groups and minorities. But instead of discarding the deliberative perspective entirely, Young suggests including alternative forms of communication such as greeting, rhetoric, and storytelling in public deliberation because they "supplement argument by providing ways of speaking across difference in the absence of significant shared understandings" (Young 1996, 129; see chapter 6 for a more thorough development of this point). Even though the deliberative paradigm puts a particular premium on fact-based reasoning in civil and respectful discussion, this does not imply that passionate and emotional public expression is seen as illegitimate and should be excluded from the discourse altogether. Rather, the deliberative perspective recognizes the benefits of these alternative forms of communication for a deliberative discourse, provided that they are eventually transformed into criticizable positions in order to realize their full persuasive effectiveness vis-à-vis the political center (Habermas 1996, 381).

Although conflicts lie at the heart of the agonistic notion of democracy, agonists do not provide much guidance with regard to their nature, origin, and possible accommodation

(Erman 2009), because agonists construe these conflicts as fundamentally irreconcilable. Agonistic models themselves offer little by way of accommodating different types of disagreement (Dryzek 2009; 2005). In particular, agonists do not provide criteria according to which one can judge which expressions and positions should be deemed democratically legitimate and which violate basic democratic norms and thus lie outside the realm of legitimate adversarial confrontation (Glover 2012).

In contrast, deliberative democratic theory has been crafted by its proponents as the normative model that most directly tackles the problems associated with intractable, moral conflicts. Central works in deliberative theory take as their starting point the facts of social pluralism and moral conflict and see moral discussion as central to political life and the original problem of democracy (e.g., Gutmann and Thompson 1996; Steiner et al. 2017). Consequently, deliberative theory has focused on how to make "distinctly moral compromises" possible by developing principles and standards for the practice of public deliberation. The underlying idea is that only such deliberation may engender genuine compromise and ensure cooperation among members of opposed moral camps (e.g., Bohman 1996). Thus, deliberative theory addresses the complexity of social reality in a more reasonable way than the agonistic perspective precisely because it is open to non-argumentative forms of communication and alternative idioms, albeit on a shared foundation of procedural fairness and commitment to justifiable solutions.

SUMMARY

The four normative models sketched here can be used as differentiated yardsticks to measure media performance. Such a multi-perspectival normative assessment

(Althaus 2012 serves to ascertain the degree to which the reality of political communication adheres to each of the normative models. Normative assessment of empirical patterns in political communication can also inform more wide-ranging discussion about which types of media democracy are desirable and which conditions are conducive to realizing them. In this context, the deliberative model developed by Habermas and refined by many other authors is the most demanding one, as it includes the exigencies of the liberal and in part also of the republican models and adds additional criteria: Compared to the liberal model, the deliberative model favors dialogic and justificatory forms of communication that can spawn reasoned dissent rather than any kind of majority opinion. With respect to the republican model, the deliberative tradition prizes camp-bridging, external contestation rather than "enclave deliberation" (Sunstein 2007) among the like-minded. The agonistic model, finally, favors distinctly different forms of communication (narrative, self-expression, etc.) that cannot be positioned on a more-or-less scale vis-à-vis deliberative exchanges. This serves as a reminder that deliberative theory should systematically study the deliberation-enhancing potential of non-argumentative forms of mediated communication and integrate them into a broader analytical scheme – a task that we will return to in chapter 6. But first we turn from the level of normative models to empirical investigations of communication in the public sphere and compare the deliberative potential of political news and discussion media both offline and online.

RECOMMENDED READING

Baker, E. C. (2002). *Media, markets, and democracy*. Cambridge University Press, Cambridge, pp. 129–54.

Dahlberg, L. (2011) "Re-constructing digital democracy: An outline of four 'positions'," *New Media & Society*, 13(6), pp. 855–72. doi: 10.1177/1461444810389569.

Ferree, M. M., Gamson, W. A., Gerhards, J., and Rucht, D. (2002) *Shaping abortion discourse: Democracy and the public sphere in Germany and the United States*. Cambridge University Press, Cambridge, pp. 205–31.

5

DELIBERATIVE QUALITIES OF NEWS
AND DISCUSSION MEDIA

It is striking that Habermas does not have great expectations of genuine deliberation *in* the media. On the contrary, he maintains that "media-based mass communication [does not need] to resemble the demanding communicative design of discourses if it is to promote deliberative politics" (Habermas 2009b, 158). Habermas reserves a less demanding role for the mass media, namely "that relevant issues and controversial answers, requisite information and appropriate arguments for and against will be mobilized" (Habermas 2009b, 162). In the system of deliberative politics, the mass media are thus supposed to inform audiences about relevant issues, and aggregate alternative positions on these issues. As we have seen in chapter 3, the core value of his theory of deliberation – argumentative exchange – is not something that should be expected from the mass media. In Habermas's view, argumentative exchange should happen in institutional contexts such as parliamentary debates, courts, or cabinet meetings instead.

Of course, this view has a lot of *prima facie* evidence in its favor. Speakers in the mediated public sphere, while talking to each other, primarily attempt not to persuade each other but to make a good impression on their audiences, which might then accept a speaker's position or argumentation in its own opinion-making process. This triadic structure – two speakers and an audience – curtails opportunities for deliberative exchanges between speakers oriented to mutual understanding, and rewards strategic communication efforts to secure support in a speaker's own camp instead (Peters 2008c, 239). In addition, this line of argument is in accordance with approaches that want to reserve the concept of mediated deliberation to mediated small-group settings, that is, to online forums specifically designed to facilitate argumentative exchanges and deliberative consultation among small numbers of participants (see Stromer-Galley and Wichowski 2011).

In contrast to this more restricted view, I advocate a *broader and more gradual conception of mediated deliberation* that looks at media discourse "in the wild" rather than specifically designed deliberative spaces (Wessler 2008; Rinke 2016). "Mediated deliberation" should be disaggregated into a set of distinct deliberative standards, which can then be used to measure the degree of media deliberativeness empirically. Such a gradual approach acknowledges that most forms of mediated communication – be it in the mass or network media – do not constitute fully deliberative, argumentative exchanges. After all, the idea of different degrees of deliberativeness presupposes that the ideal-typical argumentative exchange will be more or less strictly approximated in different media forums. But why does it make sense to keep the concept of mediated deliberation open for such gradualness rather than reserving it for the positive endpoint of the deliberativeness continuum?

The main reason is that gradual differences in deliberative performance make a big difference to the quality of democracy. Whether media users learn something substantial from mediated political communication that helps them make up their minds politically depends on, for example, whether citizens can hear all voices or only a narrow set, whether journalists clearly pinpoint the alternative positions or blur them, whether they elicit justifications from speakers or put up with unquestioned pronouncements, and whether speakers shout at each other or listen and respect diverging opinions and justifications. Different media forums have specific strengths and weaknesses with respect to one or the other of these criteria of deliberativeness. In addition, not all criteria can necessarily be maximized together, so that specific trade-offs emerge that are highly consequential for what a particular media forum can contribute to democracy.

For example, a TV talk show can reasonably be expected to show responsiveness between speakers, that is, speakers actually answering the host's questions and reacting to other speakers' utterances. In comparison, print and online news are at first sight less well suited for responsive debate but can potentially include a wider set of speaker types and more justification of opinions, due to longer texts. Microblogs like Twitter, in turn, may facilitate direct exchanges between politicians and citizens that are not commonly available in mass media forums, but offer little room for explicit justification due to the character limit for individual tweets.

In addition to such media differences the realization of deliberative standards even within one media forum varies across political and cultural contexts. In more polarized contexts such as the United States in the era of Donald Trump, Twitter will be used for less civil and less argumentative exchanges than, for example, in more consensus-oriented contexts like much of Northern Europe (for similar arguments on country differences, see Wessler and Rinke 2014; Nir 2012). Whatever the specific gradual media and country differences in deliberative performance may be, they matter because the relative dominance of a specific media forum in a specific context and historical situation means that the strengths and weaknesses of that forum will impinge on the democratic value of political communication in that context and situation. This impact on the quality of democracy can only be detected when deliberative performance is assessed gradually and the concept of deliberation is not restricted to the positive end of the continuum.

Despite obvious media (and country) differences, researchers have not yet developed a full-fledged comparative scheme of media-specific levels of deliberative performance. In fact, empirical investigations into the degree to which deliberative standards are actually being followed in mediated discourse constitute an important application of Habermas's concept of deliberative democracy.

CRITERIA OF DELIBERATIVENESS

About one hundred pieces of scholarly literature have explicitly used any criterion of deliberativeness to measure the performance of any kind of media product or forum (for an overview, see Rinke 2016). Many of these studies directly refer to aspects of Habermas's work, but others do not, and thus contribute to the state of the art more indirectly. In this chapter I offer a structured overview of the empirical literature on *media deliberativeness* in four types of media forums, namely quality newspapers, television news, Twitter, and political blogs (see table 5.1). I will not review what we know in general about the content of these media forums. Thus most of what has been written about, say, protest organization on Twitter or the tabloidization of news will not be covered here. Instead I focus on studies that measure specific elements of deliberative performance related to inclusiveness, responsiveness, justification, and civility. I aim at leveling out the manifold conceptual and operational differences in order to obtain a consolidated picture of the prospects for deliberativeness in different news and discussion media.[1] The following four criteria will be used.

1 *Inclusiveness:* Deliberative democratic theory is particularly concerned with the openness of debate. No contentious issue should be permanently suppressed and the range of voices should not be structurally curtailed (Ferree et al. 2002, 232–6; Gastil 2008, 52). By opening up public debate, news and discussion media should redress some of the inequalities in media access that exist because actors command different levels of resources to express their views publicly. Concerning the range of different voices heard it is particularly important for Habermas (1996, 359–87) that powerful actors from the center of the political system are supplemented by actors from the periphery such as civil society organizations, experts, and ordinary citizens. Attached to this criterion is the expectation that the top-down, routine mode of political decision-making be reversed every now and then and societal concerns be channeled "upward" into the political power center. In addition to the center–periphery dimension some researchers are also concerned with the composition of the speaker set in terms of gender, class, and race or ethnic group. In each case deliberative theorists favor a more even distribution of men and women, of different classes, and between majority and minority groups.

2 *Responsiveness:* Deliberative theory clearly privileges debate over monologue. A necessary condition for debate is the presence of opposing positions or claims in a media forum.

While this criterion is certainly shared with the liberal model (see chapter 4), the deliberative tradition is distinct in valuing direct responses, in which a speaker substantively engages with another speaker's position and reasons (see, for example, Bennett et al. 2004). Direct substantive responses can potentially segregate compelling from untenable arguments, according to deliberative theory (Peters 2008c, 240). In addition, deliberative theory favors an egalitarian structure of debate. Many different speakers should be heard and addressed rather than a few "power debaters" doing all the talking and commanding all the attention from others.

3 *Justification:* Mediated debates become more valuable for participants and audiences when speakers accompany their claims with justifications (Chambers 2010). In professional news media this criterion demands that journalists obtain reasons from speakers, particularly from actors in the center of the political system, for their claims and decisions and make these accessible for public contestation (Ettema 2007). This ensures the public accountability of power-holders and can serve to confer legitimacy on them if the reasons are compelling. In online discussion media, the justification criterion means that all participants should be ready to offer reasons, demand reasons from others, and question the justifications they encounter.

4 *Civility:* Theories that place deliberation at the center of the democratic process recognize that civility in mutual engagement is a necessary condition for varied positive consequences of exposure to disagreement (e.g., Mansbridge 1983; Mutz 2006) – a recognition that has been shown to apply to mediated engagements as well (e.g., Mutz 2015). The civility norm is not designed to exclude and dismiss marginalized actors and concerns from public discourse. On the contrary, it is designed to

ward off dogmatic positions and styles of communication. It is an antidote to forms of expression that immunize themselves against criticism and purely serve to gain or preserve power. Uncivil communication implicitly denies other speakers the moral right or the competence to speak legitimately on an issue (Papacharissi 2004), and it is this intolerance on the part of the uncivil speaker against which the civility norm is directed. Uncivil communication ranges from passive disrespect (e.g., sternly ignoring a particular actor, group, or concern) all the way to actively attacking other speakers (name-calling, stigmatization, insult, etc.).

The overview in table 5.1 allows for both a vertical reading that shows the distinct profile of each kind of media forum and a horizontal assessment that compares the different forums' performance levels on a particular criterion of deliberativeness. Newspapers and television news are audience media in the sense that deliberation takes place *in front of* an audience that is mostly confined to listening, watching, or reading. Twitter exchanges and political blogs are participant media designed to activate users as both speakers and listeners. For audience media the quality of deliberation is assessed on the basis of the product that audiences receive; for participant media the deliberative performance of participants' own communicative behavior is assessed.

Media affordances denote specific opportunities for action (or communication, in this case) determined by the basic characteristics of a media technology and media application (Evans et al. 2016). Affordances thus enable or constrict a particular type of use. Results from empirical studies can reveal the typical performance level found for a particular criterion and can thus inform our understanding of media

Table 5.1 Levels of deliberative performance in different media

	Quality newspapers	Television news	Twitter	Political blogs
Inclusiveness	*Egalitarian social composition*	Moderate	Moderate	Moderate	Moderate
Responsiveness	*Substantive engagement*	Moderate	Weak	Weak	Moderate
	Egalitarian structure of user debate	None	None	Weak	Weak
Justification		Strong	Moderate	Weak	Moderate
Civility		Strong	Strong	Moderate	Moderate

affordances. Performance levels are, however, not identical with media affordances, as we can easily see from the sometimes remarkable variance in performance for the same type of media forum. For example, Wessler and Rinke (2014) have shown that television news programs in different types of democracy such as the US, Germany, and Russia scarcely vary in their civility (they feature only very few acts of incivility), but differ greatly in the level of justification they provide, ranging from 10 percent of utterances containing a justification in one program to almost 50 percent in another. Both the range of performance levels and the absolute value for the top performer are instructive here. The smaller the range in different instances of the same media forum type, the more media technologies predetermine performance levels. Conversely, the wider that range turns out to be, the more additional factors such as the organizational form of the media outlet influence deliberative performance. For example, the technology of television news production offers opportunities for quite different courses of action that relate to the social organization of television news, that is, to whether we look at a commercial, a public-service, or a state-owned station.

But the absolute performance values are important, too. The value that the top performer achieves on a given criterion gives us an indication about the more general deliberative potential of the specific media forum, because it shows how closely the respective normative ideal can be approximated under real-world conditions. Of course, better conditions can in principle be created that might lead to even higher performance levels. But for the time being, if we choose a wide range of examples to study, the top performer represents a best practice model. What, then, do we learn about media's deliberative potential from the empirical studies available?

QUALITY NEWSPAPERS

Quality newspapers have historically evolved as a medium for public debate directed at the educated strata of society. As we have seen in chapter 1, the media of the early bourgeois public sphere that Habermas studied (and idealized) in his *Structural transformation of the public sphere* were largely newspapers of this kind. The "penny press" (i.e., tabloid newspapers) directed at the lower classes is a much later development, dating from the late nineteenth century, when literacy became more widespread in industrialized societies. Quality newspapers are "leading media" (Jarren and Vogel 2011) in the sense that they are read by the political, economic, and cultural elites and that their reporting and commentary exert an influence on what other media report about, a process referred to as inter-media agenda-setting (Golan 2006).

Quality newspapers have a remarkable potential for deliberativeness. They typically construct relatively *inclusive* debates around public issues that give voice to actors both from the center of the political system and from its periphery. Civil society actors are sometimes present, expert knowledge and judgment are often drawn in, and public intellectuals are being heard (Peters 2008c, 94–9). Newspapers in different countries vary somewhat in the degree to which they construct debates that talk *about* those affected by a problem or, alternatively, debates *with* them, giving some voice to ordinary citizens (or even non-citizens) who lack organizational affiliation and resources to recommend them for media coverage (see Benson 2013). Letters to the editor and forum pages offer dedicated spaces to draw in citizen opinion (Wahl-Jorgensen 2001). On the whole, coverage in quality newspapers often provides a combination of center and periphery actors, of institutional and unaffiliated actors, and thus a relatively diverse actor set even though they clearly are not egalitarian in gender, class, or racial/ethnic terms. Being audience media, the kind of *responsiveness* that newspapers mostly provide is between the actors presented in the articles. Journalistic styles vary: In traditional Anglo-American journalism "debate-style articles" are common, which juxtapose utterances from opposing sides (Ferree et al. 2002), while in continental European journalism individual articles are more often one-sided, but sometimes embedded in "debate ensembles" (Benson 2013) that distribute the opposing voices over different articles and types of text. It is rare that opposing arguments are included in the same utterance. This speaks to the incentives at work in debates presented in front of an audience, which clearly discourage the display of hesitation and uncertainty. Actors are propelled to act as if they always knew what to think and do about an issue. Bridge-builders, actors who support and weigh arguments from both sides of a controversy (Wessler 1999, 205), are few and far between. Letters to the editor are an additional tool to create responsiveness with audience members, but in print newspapers they are few and typically selected by discerning journalists for the novelty of the arguments they advance. Online newspapers in principle offer more space for any kind of content, including reader comments on articles, which constitute a separate genre of public discussion. In general, however, in print and online newspapers responsiveness is heavily constructed by journalists who allocate speaking opportunities and thus shape the confines of the debate.

This constructedness of debate in newspapers, while curtailing free-flowing responses, turns into a strength when it comes to the criterion of *justification*. Studies found that on average two fifths of the utterances made or reported on in quality newspapers contain a justification (Gerhards,

Neidhardt, and Rucht 1998; Kuhlmann 1999; Cinalli and O'Flynn 2014). Experts as well as journalists provide the highest justification rates, going up to 60–70 percent of utterances. Readers can thus not only take note of the claims but also appreciate the reasons advanced by actors in newspaper discourse. Finally, due to its construction by professional journalists, quality newspaper discourse is generally quite *civil* (Ferree et al. 2002). Utterances that disrespect, personally attack, or denigrate other actors are quite rare, and if they occur, quality newspapers tend to expose rather than just magnify them.

On the whole, therefore, quality newspapers produce a discourse that is only moderately inclusive and responsive, but highly justificatory and civil. This is obviously one of the reasons why Habermas (2009b) often publishes pieces in such outlets himself to intervene in current political debate, and openly defends the institution of the quality daily and weekly. Quality newspapers also provide an established forum for public debate with relatively similar characteristics across countries. On the other hand, quality newspapers are in danger. The business model they have relied on for a long time – subscription and retail fees plus income from consumer advertising and classified ads – is crumbling, particularly in the United States, because freely available online content has driven subscriptions down and advertising has moved to the web. In this situation, a discussion has developed in both academia and the wider public about alternative business models for quality information. In his essay on "The quality press as the backbone of the political public sphere" Habermas (2009a) contemplates selective press subsidies handed out by the state, a policy that exists in Scandinavia and France to protect smaller, less profitable newspapers and thereby secure diversity of opinion.

TELEVISION NEWS

With the proliferation of different program formats it has become quite difficult to define what television news actually looks like. In the early days of television, news was presented by an anchor either reading out short items illustrated by still images in the background or announcing video reports, which typically combine footage of events with voice-over or on-camera comments by a reporter. This traditional fact-centered type of news program has been superseded by various forms of often longer, more focused, in-depth news magazines, in which a smaller number of topics is treated in a larger variety of journalistic forms, ranging from video reports through more personal comments by the host all the way to live interviews, sometimes with two or three opponents at the same time. One prime example of such a magazine format is CNN's *Anderson Cooper 360°*.

Compared to quality newspapers, which are mostly commercial enterprises, television stations and networks feature different organizational types with diverging imperatives (Wessler and Rinke 2014). In established democracies, two models prevail: commercial stations largely financed by advertising aired between program segments on the one hand, and public-service providers financed by some combination of license fees (tax-like mandatory contributions from audiences), donations, state subsidies, and limited forms of advertising on the other. In defective democracies and authoritarian regimes, state control over TV stations is the rule. It varies in strength and can take the form of direct ownership and control or of more indirect forms of intimidation that lead to self-censorship on the part of journalists. Under such conditions deliberative performance is generally lower than in established democracies.

Wessler and Rinke (2014) provide an in-depth analysis of the levels of deliberativeness in the TV news programs in two established democracies (the USA and Germany) and one defective democracy (Russia) that has meanwhile turned into a consolidated autocracy. Figure 5.1 shows the results for the eleven programs studied. Measurement points positioned close to the perimeter of the graph indicate good deliberative performance on the respective criterion; points located toward the center denote poor performance. As a rule of thumb, therefore, the bigger the area enclosed by the jagged line, the more deliberative is the program; the smaller the area, the less deliberative.

Of the thirteen criteria studied by Wessler and Rinke (2014), eight are aligned with the criteria of deliberativeness we look at here.

- *Inclusiveness* is measured by the share of utterances originating from (a) citizens and experts (i.e. civil society actors not speaking for organizations), (b) civil society actors (i.e. the periphery of the political system), and (c) members of the political opposition in the respective country at the time of study. For citizens and experts as well as civil society in general, commercial channels like RTL, ABC, and CNN score high; while the political opposition is given stronger voice on public-service channels (PBS and ARD). In Russia, a clear divide emerged between the two state-run channels (Pervy and Rossiya24) that almost exclusively focus on state representatives, and the semi-autonomous commercial station REN that (at the time of investigation) used to give some voice to civil society and the small political opposition that exists in the Russian system.
- *Responsiveness* is operationalized as (a) the presentation of opposing positions in the same news items, and (b) the share of utterances that respond directly to another actor

(a) USA

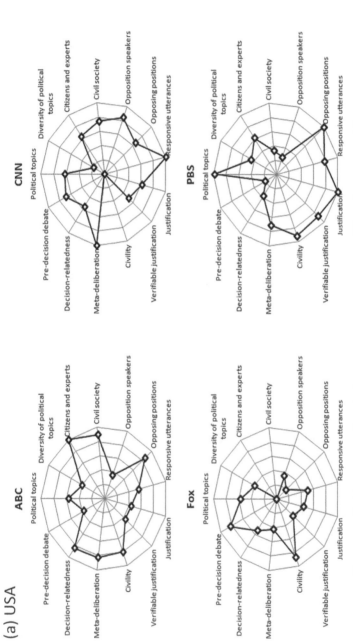

Figure 5.1 Deliberative profiles of television news programs in the USA, Germany, and Russia

Radar plots are based on the data provided in Wessler and Rinke (2014). The points displayed in the radar charts are min–max-normalized values of the original data; the formula used is: (original value–MIN)/(MAX–MIN). If the respective newscast holds the minimum value on a particular criterion the dot is placed in the middle of the chart; maximum values are placed on the outer margin.

(b) Germany

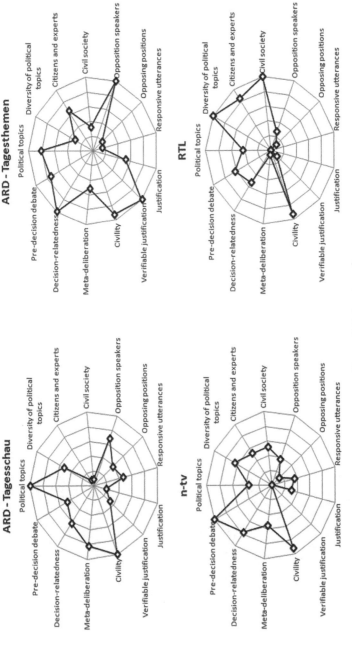

Figure 5.1 (continued)

(c) Russia

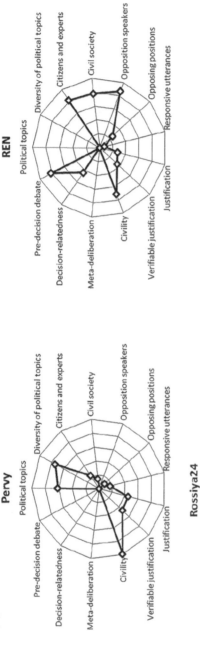

Figure 5.1 (continued)

or utterance. Actors do address each other in television news, but substantive engagement with other positions is mostly low. The American channels (ABC, CNN, and PBS) – with the clear exception of the conservative-leaning Fox News – are somewhat more responsive than the German and Russian ones, indicating that the norm of juxtaposing and relating opposing positions is still alive in US mainstream television news.

- *Justification* is determined by the share of claims-making utterances that (a) contain any kind of reason for the claim, and (b) contain reasons that can in principle be verified (like empirical facts, etc.). The focused, in-depth news magazines offered by the public-service stations PBS and ARD as well as by CNN – and again not the news magazine on Fox News – come out as front-runners on this account.

- Finally, *civility* is measured by its opposite, the share of utterances that contain insulting language or derogatory gestures. There is very little variation here. Television news is generally very civil; even the outlier, CNN, features only 2 percent uncivil utterances.

Disregarding the variation on each dimension for a moment, we can conclude that television news discourse scores moderately regarding inclusiveness and justification, weakly regarding responsiveness, and highly with regard to civility. Journalists' preference for institutional actors makes it more difficult for civil society actors to gain attention in television news than in newspapers. But civil society is by no means absent from TV news in established democracies. As a largely non-interactive genre, television news does not prompt many direct responses between actors. Television news creates a streamlined, civil, partly elite-driven type of discourse that makes diverging positions transparent to some degree, but does not offer responsive engagement most of the time. A healthy deliberative media diet would therefore have to include additional offerings that allow for more responsive debate such as online discussion boards, blogs, or microblogs, to which we now turn.

TWITTER

Twitter allows users to post short tweets, for which the character limit allowed has been extended from the original 140 to 280. This is combined with a social network component by which users can follow other users unilaterally and are thus shown these other users' (algorithmically selected and prioritized) tweets on their Twitter home screen. In the following we look at a number of Twitter features that are decisive for the level of Twitter's potential to facilitate deliberative exchanges.

First, Twitter users can organize tweets thematically by using *hashtags* (e.g., #deliberation); users can also search for a hashtag and are then shown all tweets containing it. Hashtags provide spontaneous user-generated coherence in the universe of tweets, but sometimes different camps in a debate choose to tweet under different hashtags, so that it is not always clear whether a hashtag captures the full range of positions or a selective segment of a particular debate. Second, tweets can be addressed to specific Twitter users by using the @ *function* within the character limit. The @ function is used to either directly address or respond to another user or to mention another user so that that person will see the tweet. This offers potential for interaction or at least mutual information about who posted what. Twitter users can also write private messages to each other, but since these cannot be seen by other users they do not directly support public debate. Third, tweets may contain photos or videos in addition to the short text or they may contain links to other resources on the Internet. The additional resources may serve different functions in relation to the tweet, some of which might support justification; for example, when the resource provides evidentiary support for a claim made in a tweet or when a longer text on a website gives a more elaborate argument. Finally, Twitter users can choose to retweet other people's tweets. The embedded retweet button gives the unaltered tweet enhanced circulation by making it visible to the followers of the retweeting user. But the user can also choose to edit the tweet before retweeting it, for example to mention an additional addressee or to link the tweet to an additional hashtag or resource, or in order to criticize the claim ("manual retweet"). Retweets are not automatically considered to be endorsements of the original tweet. Users can also retweet to expose or ridicule a tweet whose claim they oppose. Twitter also offers the option to express endorsement through liking a tweet.

At first sight these Twitter features may seem ideal for facilitating inclusive and responsive debate, particularly between ordinary citizens and politicians, although opportunities for justification seem more limited as users have to click on links to view supportive material beyond the 280 characters, and the logical relation of the material to the claim remains implicit. What, then, do we know empirically about the deliberativeness of Twitter exchanges?

The answer to this question is complicated by the fact that studies of Twitter rarely look at deliberative qualities directly. Many existing studies are concerned with the potential of Twitter to mobilize for and organize protest, which is of course not identical with deliberation. And in the case of responsiveness, justification, and civility, measures of deliberativeness must be altered to fit the peculiarities of Twitter. For example, suppose that a Twitter conversation features many *responsive* tweets that address others or manually retweet other people's claims. At face value, this would indicate a high degree of deliberativeness. But if in a particular debate those responsive tweets are mostly sucked up by very few actors with high levels of "indegree centrality" (i.e. attracting large numbers of directly addressed tweets using @ or other people's manual retweets), then the deliberative benefit of those responsive tweets is lost to the debate at large. The debate would then just be strongly centered on a few powerful figures, but not characterized by broad, inclusive discussion. When proportion measures (responsive tweets) and network features are combined in appropriate ways, the analysis comes much closer to Habermas's original intuition about public deliberation being a macro-societal process of debate. However, Twitter's network structure imposes strong restrictions on true reciprocity in such debate. Unlike Facebook, where friendship relations require the consent of both users, Twitter users follow others unilaterally. This built-in asymmetry makes responsive debate between many users unlikely from the outset.

Second, *justifications* presuppose the existence of a claim. When a claim is made within a tweet, we can distinguish two types of justification: Internal justifications are given in the body of the tweet and external justifications are provided via a link to some external resource. Freelon (2015) shows that internal justification is very rare on Twitter. According to Himelboim, McCreery, and Smith (2013) and Jungherr (2014), about three fifths to two thirds of tweets have an external link. However, it is unclear how many of these links perform a justificatory function.

Finally, Twitter debates often exhibit special forms of *incivility*. Derogatory comments that use swear words, upper-case characters, or exclamation marks, for example, constitute "flaming" (Shephard 2014). They are akin to uncivil utterances in offline media. But some users also engage in "trolling," an attempt to disrupt the discussion without any systematic substantive contribution (Buckels, Trapnell, and Paulhus 2014), or "spamming," that is, obstructing communication by flooding it with unrelated and distracting content (Shin, Gupta, and Myers 2011). By refraining from these forms of communication Twitter users show respect toward the integrity of public discussion itself, if not toward the other participants more directly. Civility on Twitter thus comprises both of these elements.

What level of deliberative performance, then, is suggested by the existing studies on Twitter debates? First, such debates do contain large shares of tweets from actors belonging to the *periphery* of the political system. Percentages can range around 50 percent and more (Ausserhofer and Maireder 2013; Graham et al. 2013; Öncü and Abele 2015) and peripheral voices are particularly important in the early phases of mobilization (Jackson and Foucault Welles 2016). However, the majority of tweets from the periphery take the form of retweets, dampening hopes for the active inclusion of individual citizens in mediated debate. Twitter discussions also often display a power law distribution, with few users issuing large shares of tweets (Tumasjan et al. 2011) and attracting most tweets from others (Öncü and Abele 2015). This unequal structure of debate can offset the benefits of the many *responsive* tweets (ranging from 10 up to 50 percent of tweets) because it implies that less central actors in the network are less well connected among each other. In addition, the large numbers of ordinary citizens and actors from the political periphery in Twitter networks are not necessarily included in actual interaction with center actors. Politicians seem to use Twitter more often to disseminate their opinions and achievements than to engage in meaningful discussion with citizens. This trend is only aggravated by the more recent use of social bots on Twitter, which auto-matically multiply the same messages over and over.

In the confines of 280 characters not much explicit *justi-fication* can be realized, so that external resources are crucial. But the possible justificatory relationship between tweets and external resources has not been properly assessed to date; consequently Twitter's justification levels are some-what unclear, but probably rather low. Finally, different studies find somewhat divergent levels of *incivility* in Twitter debates, ranging below 15 percent. In part, this is likely due to the fact that Twitter applies filtering algorithms that delete some inflammatory posts as well as spam. But shit storms do happen on Twitter like on other social media platforms.

The overall picture is thus mixed: Twitter offers the potential for vertical interaction between actors from the political periphery and the center, and for direct respon-sive engagement not available in mass media forums. On the other hand, this potential is thwarted by elite-centered network structures in many debates that minimize interac-tion between less central actors. In addition, the potential for justification seems quite low and incivility occurs more often than in most offerings mediated by professional journalists. Twitter therefore has somewhat limited capacities for delib-erative exchanges.

POLITICAL BLOGS

Blogs are web offerings that arrange individual postings in reverse chronological order. Blog posts are typically longer than tweets and may run to several paragraphs. Most blogs enable users to comment on posts as well as on previous comments by other users. Apart from these basic technical features, however, blogs – and political blogs in particular – take quite different institutional forms. Some political blogs are written by professional journalists, who can use their blogs to express themselves more personally and subjectively than they do in the media outlet for which they work. Others are maintained by academic experts or think tanks not affiliated to media outlets. Still others are produced by political action groups or nongovernmental organizations supporting particular causes or candidates. Finally, non-professional writers such as interested citizens also maintain political blogs. Most political blogs are opinion-oriented rather than strictly fact-based.

Political blogospheres differ markedly from one country to another. They develop in relation to the existing system of political communication and serve functions complementary to what already exists. In the United States, for example, political blogs have emerged as an important new layer of political contestation relatively independent from the mainstream media and political party communication (Hyun 2012). This is related to a tradition of direct citizen involvement in the US, whereas in European countries a culture of organizationally mediated interest articulation is stronger (Hallin and Mancini 2004; Wessler 2008) and thus individual blogging is less salient (Eckert, Chadha, and Koliska 2014). In addition, political blogging in the United States displays a clearer left/right division, with bloggers on both sides of the political spectrum predominantly linking to like-minded others rather than engaging in camp-bridging contestation (Sunstein 2007). Conversely, in Germany and the UK political blogs are both less popular and influential overall and less fiercely polarized (Hyun 2012). In authoritarian contexts, political blogs do provide opportunities for dissenting voices excluded from the state-run media, but of course their leeway and influence depend heavily on the level of surveillance and state prosecution they encounter (Etling et al. 2010a; 2010b).

In terms of *inclusiveness*, Hindman (2010) shows for the late 1990s that the blogs in the US can indeed be called "the new elite media," as most of the political top bloggers were educated at elite institutions, some are or were professional journalists, all belong to a highly privileged stratum of society, and all but one were male. Ordinary citizens typically make up the long tail of blogs less widely read. Demographically, influential bloggers do not differ much from those who write for quality newspapers. Bloggers create *responsive* exchanges in several ways. They can refer to the writing of other bloggers in their own blogposts, or they can post comments on other blogs and thus engage with their opinions (Koop and Jansen 2009). Most links in blogposts, however, refer to mainstream media content that bloggers comment on. When bloggers in the US refer to each other, nine out of ten references are to blogs of the same political leaning; only 10 percent reach across the political divide (Hargittai, Gallo, and Kane 2008). Most of these camp-bridging references are critical, sometimes mocking or ridiculing the other side. Shaw and Benkler (2012) show that among the US top political blogs about 20 percent feature predominantly argumentative posts and adopt a style of substantive discussion. This is the closest estimate of the level of *justification* in political blogs found in the existing literature. Concerning *civility*, there are indications that blogs are more civil on average than tweets, at least when we consider top blogs, but a large shadow area remains in the long tail. On the whole, political blogs are as inclusive as Twitter debates, or maybe even less so, but offer a greater potential for justifying claims. The dominance of a few political top bloggers attracting most of the traffic from blog readers makes blogs as non-egalitarian in their debate structure as Twitter.

SUMMARY

What are the strong and the weak spots in the deliberativeness of news and discussion media? When we review table 5.1, the strongest deliberative potential seems to reside in traditional quality newspapers, particularly as they offer room for the justification of claims and for civil exchange. Television news is also generally very civil. Interestingly, weak spots can be found in the non-egalitarian structure of online debates, be they on Twitter or in the blogosphere, where the absence of professional journalistic mediation means that debates can become strongly centered on a few dominant speakers. This finding runs counter to overly optimistic accounts of cyberdemocracy involving everyone. Of course, in newspapers and TV news there is no visible user debate at all, which is even worse. In addition, due to format restrictions Twitter offers little possibility for speakers to substantiate and justify their claims in an argumentative fashion. And television news is generally weak in creating substantive engagement with opposing positions.

Of course, one can argue that it is not the purpose of television news to imitate talk shows, and that a microblogging platform like Twitter was not designed to offer lengthy argumentation. This is true. But it is still highly instructive to monitor the strengths and weaknesses of various media forums in realizing particular aspects of Habermas's deliberative ideals. And a few myths can be discarded along the way. One such myth has it that online media are generally more suitable for deliberative democracy than mass media. When we look at how they are actually used – rather than merely at their technical potential – their weaknesses become clear despite their strengths in certain sub-dimensions. It is striking that the oldest among the media analyzed here, the quality newspaper, carries the strongest deliberative potential. No wonder, then, that Habermas favors the quality newspaper in his theoretical work as well as for his own engagement as a public intellectual. As media use is shifting away from quality dailies and weeklies in many of the established democracies and toward individualized diets of social-media-induced political information morsels, the prospects for mediated deliberative exchanges seem bleak; or, to put it more positively, a lot of deliberative imagination will be required to envision productive synergies between the analytical qualities of quality journalism and the potentially inclusive exchanges facilitated by online and social media.

RECOMMENDED READING

Freelon, D. (2015) "Discourse architecture, ideology, and democratic norms in online political discussion," *New Media & Society*, 17(5), pp. 772–91.

Mutz, D. C. (2015) *In-your-face-politics: The consequences of uncivil media*. Princeton University Press, Princeton, NJ.

Wessler, H. and Rinke, E. M. (2014) "Deliberative performance of television news in three types of democracy: Insights from the United States, Germany, and Russia," *Journal of Communication*, 64(5), pp. 827–51.

6

NON-DELIBERATIVE MEDIA DISCOURSE

Instances of deliberative exchange are usually embedded in non-deliberative forms of media discourse. Some would argue that the word "embedded" is euphemistic and that deliberative content is drowned in all that other stuff we find in the mass and network media. Whatever interpretation we prefer, there certainly is a tension between truly deliberative communication and non-deliberative content in the media. This tension can be resolved in two directions when we analyze media: We can either focus exclusively on the truly deliberative content we can find and normatively discard everything else. But this would leave us with little to work with in empirical analysis and would be relatively remote from people's actual media diets. Alternatively, we can include the non-deliberative forms in media analysis and consistently search for their deliberative benefits. This is the route I will pursue in this chapter.

In his own writing Habermas has not paid much attention to non-deliberative mediated communication and the wider context of cultural production. His main concern clearly lies in offering a universal grounding for deliberative communication as the archetypal form of communication based on the counterfactual presuppositions that we regularly make in everyday communication, i.e. the validity claims of truth, moral rightness, and truthfulness. Habermas does not himself study the mass or network media as important sites for communicative exchanges that display at least some level of deliberativeness or for societal learning processes. As we have seen in chapter 3, he is content with treating the media as a macro context for processes of opinion- and will-formation in both the citizenry and formal political institutions.

In looking at this macro context of the media and their output, however, he also refrains from studying in any detail those pervasive non-deliberative forms of media discourse, even though he generally acknowledges the existence of expressive and aesthetic aspects of communication (Habermas 1984, 23). Thus Habermas's work does not directly contribute a whole lot to the systematic analysis of cultural products and trends and of the societal learning processes that can be associated with them. But if his theory is to have a continuing influence on media and communication studies, this missing link can no longer be ignored. In a Habermasian spirit, therefore, we should ask:

- How can non-deliberative forms of media discourse contribute to carving out a space for genuine societal discussion in the public sphere?
- Which forms of non-deliberative media discourse are conducive and which are detrimental to such genuine discussion?
- In what way can non-deliberative media discourse contribute to collective learning processes?

These questions open up a whole new territory for productive and exciting media analysis that more fully grasps the democratic potential of the media than existing research. Deliberative democracy is seen as a large-scale context for collective learning, and the democratic potential of non-deliberative media discourse therefore lies in facilitating such society-wide discussion and learning.

In tackling the contributions of non-deliberative forms of communication and media, two layers can be distinguished. On the level of individual communicative acts in the public sphere we find non-deliberative forms of utterance firmly integrated into more deliberative exchanges. For example, Young (2000) proposes to treat "greeting" (publicly acknowledging someone as part of a conversation), rhetoric (the use of verbal and nonverbal means to produce an effect in audiences), and personal, self-revelatory narrative as integral elements of deliberation. According to Young, greeting, rhetoric, and narrative do not diminish but enhance the democratic potential of deliberation. We will come back to this argument later.

But there is a second level of analysis that comprises broad communicative approaches to the social world, which cut across different mass and network media forums and can equally foster or inhibit genuine discussion and societal learning. We will focus on three of these approaches here.

Satire, for one, epitomizes a *playful, yet critical* relation to the social world, particularly as it makes fun of or sarcastically exposes what it perceives to be stupid, self-contradictory, or immoral practices. Second, mediated protest action establishes *direct and explicit opposition* to what it sees as unjust and destructive social structures and relations. The Arab Spring, the Occupy Wall Street protests, and other social movements attest to the fact that protest is heavily imbued with media activity. Third, mediated public rituals aim at *symbolically repairing* disrupted or derailed social relations by performatively making an alternative world imaginable. We will take public reactions to the deadly attack on the French satirical magazine *Charlie Hebdo* in January 2015 as our case in point here.

More or less deliberative exchanges in the media are also broadly contextualized by other forms of cultural production – mediatized or not, and more or less overtly political – that may take on supportive roles in society-wide public discussion. Prime examples of these are fictional films and series, popular music, literature, theater, and other visual and performing arts. To keep the argument manageable we will not look at this wider cultural context in greater detail here (for an attempt in that direction, see McGuigan 2005), but focus on the levels of individual utterances on the one hand and broad communicative approaches in media discourse on the other.

WHICH DELIBERATIVE BENEFITS?

For the Habermasian media analyst the challenge lies in showing which particular elements or features of non-deliberative media discourse are conducive to genuine societal debate, that is, to the exchange of ideas and arguments in identifying and dealing with collective problems. However, non-deliberative forms of communication can contribute to different aspects of such genuine debate and social learning. These must first be disentangled (for important groundwork on this task, see Gastil 2008; Kanra 2012). The following is a list of possible contributions of non-deliberative media discourse that can occur separately or jointly depending on the character of the content.

1 *Drawing attention and enhancing interest*: The most basic step in facilitating more deliberative exchanges in the

public sphere lies in sensitizing speakers and/or audiences to a particular issue or problem and attracting their interest to it. Impassioned rhetoric and protest action can help serve this function.

2 *Adding perspectives and increasing inclusiveness*: Not only personal narratives but also protest seem well suited to giving voice to people, experiences, and perspectives that might otherwise be neglected in mediated communication.

3 *Strengthening social bonds and showing solidarity*: The public acknowledgment of other participants even if they are adversaries ("greeting"), personal narratives, protest action, and public ritual can all in their particular ways enhance social cohesion and thus contribute to building trust among participants.

4 *Highlighting values and facilitating normative problematization*: This function can be supported, for example, by personal narrative connecting individual experiences with general values; by satire and political jokes, particularly when they resist and debunk authorities that have become illegitimate; and by protest that invokes values against practices of suppression, injustice, or exclusion.

5 *Providing arguments and justifications*: Contributions to this core function of deliberation – the public exchange of reasons – can, among others, be expected from political satire and mediated protest, as these forms of discourse often furnish proto-arguments that can be further elaborated in deliberative exchanges.

6 *Offering solutions and imagining alternatives:* This creative function of deliberation is best supported by discourse that ventilates possible and imagined worlds, such as mediated protest and some forms of public ritual.

Every non-deliberative form of communication should be assessed against this list of possible contributions in order to identify the unique contributions to individual acts or societal patterns of mediated public discussion that each can make.

GREETING, RHETORIC, AND PERSONAL NARRATIVE

Several authors have described productive and supportive roles that non-deliberative communication can play for mediated discussion. James Bohman (1996) shows how social critics can set off public deliberation processes by what he calls disclosure. Disclosive communication is more than introducing new subjects. It opens up new possibilities of seeing things and thus challenges entrenched patterns of interpretation that have become rigid and can thus not satisfy deliberative majorities anymore. Disclosures also open up new possibilities for dialogue because they "are not self-justifying or self-verifying, but require public reflection to test them for idiosyncrasy. These same tests open up a new dialectic, however, between public verification of the new forms of democracy and the resistance by the older publics and its stable institutions, between older and newer forms of publicly generated power" (Bohman 1996, 229). Social critics often achieve the eye-opening effect of disclosive communication

indirectly by jokes, irony, storytelling, and other indirect forms of communication. What unites all these forms of communication is not that they raise a certain claim – say, to truth or correctness – but that the hearer comes to see things in a new way, take up a different perspective, or change attitudes. They are not merely accepted but tried and taken on, and in considering them the hearer is opened up to a new pattern of relevance – to a new perspective on what may count as potentially good reasons. (Bohman 1996, 225f.)

Iris Marion Young (2000) elaborates on this eye-opening effect by offering a three-pronged argument about the positive functions of greeting, rhetoric, and personal narrative for furthering political communication (for a summary of the ensuing controversies, see Maia 2012, 13–24). Table 6.1 summarizes the main deliberative contribution of all three communicative forms.

Greeting means publicly acknowledging others as part of the discussion and thereby taking responsibility for the mutual relationship. "The political functions of such moments of greeting are to assert discursive equality and establish or re-establish the trust necessary for discussion to proceed in good faith" (Young 2000, 60). This means that greeting is a precondition of deliberation, because without acknowledging those affected by a speaker's opinion and reasons as partners in the discussion the exchange of reasons becomes senseless. "One sign of the absence of such greeting is that a public debate across mass society refers to persons or social segments only in the third person, never addressing them in the second person" (Young 2000, 62). In media discourse this can mean, for example, including those affected by a problem in a talk show discussion or signaling readiness to listen to them in an online debate. Greeting thus supports function (3) in table 6.1 in certain ways because it strengthens social bonds between those affected by and those discussing a problem.

Rhetoric is a set of attributes that, according to Young (2000, 65), all discourse possesses. It includes the emotional tone of the discourse, the use of figurative speech (metaphors, puns, etc.), nonlinguistic forms of making a point (visuals, banners, etc.), and the orientation of the claims and arguments

Table 6.1   Potential deliberative benefits of non-deliberative utterances

	Greeting (public acknow-ledgment)	Rhetoric	Personal narrative
1 Attention and interest			
2 Additional perspectives, inclusiveness			
3 Social bonds, solidarity			
4 Values, normative problematization			
5 Arguments, justifications			
6 Solutions, imaginative alternatives			

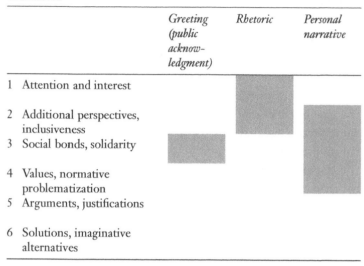

to the predilections of a particular audience. Young identifies three distinctively positive functions of rhetoric for deliberation. First, rhetoric can create attention for a neglected or silenced issue or group (function (1) in table 6.1). Second, "[r]hetoric constructs the speaker, audience, and occasion by invoking or creating specific connotations, symbols, and commitments. Through rhetoric we construct our positions and messages in a way appropriate to the particular context and audience to which we are speaking" (Young 2000, 68f.). This can be read as a contribution to including particular groups and subcultures in the conversation (akin to function (2)). Third, "[t]he situated, figured, and affective appeal of rhetoric helps make possible the move from thinking to committed action that [...] political judgement involves" (Young 2000, 69). This motivational contribution concerns the aftermath or external effect of deliberation not directly relevant here, but crucial for social action.

Despite such positive contributions, Habermas finds that rhetoric possesses a "Janus face." It oscillates between "the world-disclosing power of new vocabularies" (like Bohman said) and "the constraining, often manipulative effects of suggestive and emotionally charged metaphors" (Habermas 2009b, 151). Chambers (2009) convincingly elaborates on this Janus face by distinguishing deliberative rhetoric from plebiscitary rhetoric. "Deliberative rhetoric makes people think, it makes people see things in new ways, it conveys information and knowledge, and it makes people more reflective. [...] It ought to spark active reasoning and thoughtfulness rather than unreflective triggers and gut reactions" (Chambers 2009, 335). Plebiscitary rhetoric, on the other hand, "reigns when campaigns are vapid and vacuous, when voters are given no information, when the press only covers strategy and never policy, when politicians say anything to get elected, and finally and most importantly, when the audience, that is citizens, remains passive" (Chambers 2009, 337). Plebiscitary rhetoric comes in two main forms: pandering, i.e. politicians only telling citizens what they want to hear without wanting to persuade them; and priming, i.e. crafting messages so as to elicit support, again without substantive engagement vis-à-vis citizens. Rather than rhetoric being salvaged in general, from a Habermasian perspective it has to be evaluated on whether it invites reflection in listeners, leading them to consider their genuine preferences and the underlying reasons.

A similarly differentiated view should be applied to the third of Young's non-deliberative ingredients of deliberation: personal, self-revelatory *narrative* (see also Boswell 2013). In personal narratives, experiences can be voiced that cannot be readily translated into arguments. This can be the case either because society generally lacks a language to name the experience, as in the case of sexual harassment before the 1970s; or because the particular speaker does not command the competencies required for argumentative discourse, as in the case of some disadvantaged groups; or because in large, pluralistic societies one group does not have access to the lifeworld and experience of another group and is thus trapped in prejudice and false assumptions (Young 2000, 74). In these cases personal experiential narrative can be an antidote that (a) adds perspectives to public debates (function (2) in table 6.1), (b) creates social bonds between those making the same experiences, and (c) facilitates perspective-taking and empathy in participants not affected by the experience but confronted with it through narrative (both elements of function (3)). Furthermore, perspective-taking also extends to the realm of values (function (4)): "Values, unlike norms, often, cannot be justified through argument. But neither are they arbitrary. Their basis often emerges from the situated narrative of persons or groups. Through narrative the outsiders may come to understand why the insiders value what they value and why they have the priorities they have" (Young 2000, 75).

SATIRE, MEDIATED PROTEST, AND PUBLIC RITUAL

Satire, protest, and public rituals epitomize a subversive, an oppositional, and a restorative approach to the perceived social world, respectively. Despite their difference in approach, all three are cross-media phenomena. Political satire is a popular program element on television, particularly in the form of news parody shows, but satirical expression and political jokes also pervade the Internet, chiefly in the form of memes. Protest activities rely heavily on network media today, leading to new forms of mobilizing through "connective action" (Bennett and Segerberg 2013), even though traditional media coverage remains important for society-wide dissemination of

Table 6.2 Potential deliberative benefits of non-deliberative media content

	Satire	Mediated protest	Mediated public ritual
1 Attention and interest	■	■	
2 Additional perspectives, inclusiveness		■	■
3 Social bonds, solidarity		■	■
4 Values, normative problematization	■	■	
5 Arguments, justifications	■	■	
6 Solutions, imaginative alternatives		■	■

protest messages (Rinke and Röder 2011). Similarly, mediated public ritual has developed away from the television genre of celebratory "media events" as originally conceived by Dayan and Katz (1992) toward a hybrid product often intertwining live transmission, professional coverage, and social media fandom and debate. Table 6.2 summarizes the contributions that these three approaches can make to society-wide discussion and learning.

Satire

"What can satire do? – Anything," German journalist and satirist Kurt Tucholsky famously exclaimed in an article for the liberal daily *Berliner Tageblatt* on January 27, 1919. In this article (for which he used the pseudonym Ignaz Wrobel) and in his entire oeuvre, Tucholsky fought against what he perceived as an overly craven and submissive public culture in Germany after World War I. "When somebody makes a good joke around here, half of Germany sits on the sofa and takes offense."[1] This is a powerful reminder that in order to function well satire needs an uncontrolled and tolerant public sphere – but also one that is not indifferent or lackadaisical, lest satirical provocation run dry.

Satire comes in many shapes and colors. Horatian satire is more entertaining, light-hearted, and playful than Juvenalian satire, which can be bitter, angry, and confrontational (see Holbert et al. 2011). Tucholsky himself, again using "Ignaz Wrobel" as his pseudonym, furnished a particularly famous example of the Juvenalian bite when he wrote in the progressivist weekly *Die Weltbühne* in 1931: "Soldiers are murderers." Tucholsky had served in the German army himself during World War I and had become a staunch pacifist afterward as well as an exceptionally talented Juvenalian satirist. Tucholsky's antimilitaristic slogan was seen by many as an intolerable provocation and a lawsuit was filed against *Weltbühne*'s editor, Carl von Ossietzky, for allowing it to be published. Fortunately, Ossietzky was acquitted because the jury found that the sentence did not insult particular individuals but "villainized war," as Ossietzky had said. This jury decision attests to the fact that a less authority-fixated and craven public culture had indeed developed in Germany in the 1920s, which was, however, destroyed by the Nazi movement coming to power in 1933. It was only to resurface in Germany in the 1960s.

This example shows that Juvenalian satire was and continues to be a vital element of spirited and tolerant public discourse. In today's entertainment-saturated mediated public spheres, however, it seems that the more light-hearted Horatian satire prevails. In fact, the line that used to separate Horatian satire, or satire in general, from purely entertaining comedy seems to be blurring (Kleinen-von Königslöw and Keel 2012). Nevertheless we will focus here on forms of satire that preserve a critical edge vis-à-vis the social world.

What, then, can be the contributions of satire to genuine societal debate? Whether in its Horatian or Juvenalian form, the strength of satire lies in normative problematization (function (4) in table 6.2). Through the use of irony, human fallacies and more severe forms of misconduct are exposed and ridiculed through confrontation with the accused's self-proclaimed values or with common-sense morality (see Holbert 2013). As Bernhard Peters remarks, caricature, satire, irony, and exaggeration "can – as barbs, the medium of bitter truths, or as revelations – serve as effective means for a critical public sphere. Implicitly, such criticism makes use of argumentative foundations – but they depend upon a transfer into the realm of the discursive" (Peters 2008a, 144). The argumentative foundations that Peters finds important, if hidden, in satirical forms refer to the juxtaposition of self-proclaimed or taken-for-granted values with actual behavior or social conditions. But media debates must unearth this latent argumentative potential of satire in order to shift public debate from normative problematization to actual argumentation and justification (function (5)). Critics might take comfort in the fact that some forms of satire can contain as much substantive information on political processes as mainstream news programs do (Fox, Koloen, and Sahin 2007).

Compared to values and argumentation, satire on the whole seems to do much less to include unheard perspectives, to create social bonds, and to suggest solutions (functions (2), (3), and (6), respectively). The voice that speaks out in satire, particularly in the more playful Horatian satire, is often associated with common sense and everyday morality, rather than with a specific marginalized group or dissident perspective. So satire makes a smaller contribution to inclusiveness than protest actions by social movements, for example. As for social bonds, some have argued that certain forms of satire such as the hugely popular news parody shows already mentioned tend to destroy rather than nurture feelings of mutual commitment because they spread political cynicism (Hart 2013; Hart and Hartelius 2007). Satire is largely "negative"; it criticizes by making people laugh or by creating outrage. Its role is rarely constructive or solution-oriented – at least much less so than the role of social movements, think tanks, or even journalistic commentators. By contrast, satire can enhance attention to a problem, especially for those who do not regularly and attentively follow the news, and counterbalance omissions and distortions in the mainstream media system (Bennett 2007). By picking an issue and creating catchphrases or powerful visual depictions problematizing it, satire can lift individual concerns from the steady flow of information and popularize them (function (1)).

Mediated Protest

Is protest not by definition the prototype of agonistic rather than deliberative behavior? After all, activists and protesters unilaterally demand change from their opponents, often national governments, big business, or transnational agencies. And to be heard they engage in symbolic or performative actions that can range from using provocative banners and slogans through civil disobedience to violence. It is true that the main dividing line in protest situations is between the protesters and their opponents and that in general no deliberative stance can be expected between the two camps. Protest is about confronting or disrupting institutionalized power. But upon closer inspection, mediated protest events and movements do contribute to genuine debate both internally, within the group of protesters, and externally, triggering debate in the news media and among decision-makers.

Focusing on internal deliberation in the protest camp, Min (2015) offers a telling example based on his participant observation of the Occupy Wall Street protests in the US. In the movement's "General Assemblies," participants "were addicted to the procedural ideals of participatory democracy. It was as if they took a playbook from Jürgen Habermas's massive work in communicative action and deliberation, and put the demanding theory into real actions" (Min 2015, 74). They used the "human mic" technique to discuss in large groups of a hundred people or more, collectively repeating individual contributions sentence by sentence and thus forcing participants to audibly voice statements that they sometimes disagreed with. "I *had to* verbally repeat the things that I didn't approve of. At the same time, however, that was the moment that I had a feeling of a shared connection to the group. These excruciatingly slow speech acts over the human mic made the discussants more reflexive, facilitating them to assess their identities and to carefully evaluate others' arguments" (Min 2015, 78). This description clearly speaks to creating social bonds between participants and to engaging in real argumentative debate by closely listening to arguments that participants disagreed with initially (functions (3) and (5) in table 6.2). Min also argues that the Occupy protests more broadly served as a symbol of how democracy should be working, a *role model* that provides normative orientation and inspires and sustains democratic grassroots initiative. Protest thus also helps imagine alternatives to actually existing political routines (function (6)).

Beyond such internal deliberative benefits, protest can under favorable conditions also spur external debate in both the news media and decision-making bodies. For one thing, it can serve to propel neglected issues and taboos onto the media agenda and, by implication, also onto citizens' and politicians' agendas (Habermas 1996, 381ff.; Min 2015) (function (1)). Protest challenges and problematizes routines of exclusion and makes the demands of the excluded visible and audible (functions (2) and (4)). It can also entice additional actors such as experts or intellectuals or civil society groups not directly affiliated with the protest action to speak out on the issue highlighted by the protesters, thus creating a more wide-ranging societal debate and sometimes dominating a society's issue agenda for some time.

Under favorable conditions protests might also trigger genuine debate on the part of the power-holders they challenge. Government representatives can decide to heed some of the protestors' demands, thus establishing a genuine dialogue with them on the merits of their proposals either directly or through announcements in the media, for example in television interviews or the like (Mendonça and Ercan 2015). Of course, such government concessions can also serve to simply deflect some of the pressure and then let things continue as before, but there is no automatism here. Government and political opposition might also enter into institutional deliberations about policy changes, with the parliamentary opposition sometimes echoing the calls of the protestors and transforming their demands into concrete legal provisions or proposals for the allocation of public funds. The deliberativeness of such subsequent institutional deliberation depends on the long-term character of the political discourse culture in a given context (Peters 2008a, 246; Hepp and Wessler 2009) as well as on the short-term discursive opportunity structures (Ferree et al. 2002) that the protests create. Together they provide (or fail to provide) incentives for political actors to engage in dialogue with their opponents. Of course the success of mediated protest in creating favorable societal debate that leads to actual political change is highly contingent. But as such, protest seems quite potent to affect societal discussion in all the aspects highlighted in table 6.2.

Mediated Public Ritual

On January 7, 2015, Islamist terrorists launched a deadly attack in Paris on the editorial team of the satirical magazine *Charlie Hebdo*, on a kosher supermarket, and on law enforcement officers. These events sent a wave of shock, outrage, and solidarity through France and across the world. "Je suis Charlie" became the slogan of major demonstrations and newspaper editorials, and was used as a Twitter hashtag and Facebook profile picture by many users. (The *Charlie Hebdo* assassins were killed in a police operation a few days after the attack, but the terror in France did not end, with an even greater excess of deadly violence on November 13, 2015, when several groups of Islamist terrorists simultaneously killed 130 people in Paris, and the attack in Nice on July 14, 2016, which claimed 86 lives.)

Following the *Charlie Hebdo* attack there were spontaneous demonstrations of grief and solidarity in Paris and many other cities on the evening of January 7, 2015, and the following days. The largest demonstration, however, was the so-called Republican March, which brought 1.5 million people onto the streets in Paris on Sunday, January 11. As part of the Republican March, President François Hollande organized a public appearance of forty-four heads of state or government from around the world. According to Hollande's explicit wish, Mali's president Ibrahim Boubacar Keïta marched on his right and German Chancellor Angela Merkel on his left. Israel and several Muslim countries were also represented by their top officials. The march of the heads of state was conducted and filmed in a side street due to security reasons, but presented by many media outlets as if it had been a part of the big citizens' march. This tacit, if incorrect, montage was later censured by some media critics. But its occurrence shows that both government officials and mainstream media collaborated in sending a signal of faith-bridging solidarity – an instance of public ritual well captured by Dayan and Katz's (1992) theory of celebratory media events. The participation of officials from several countries that disrespect the freedom of expression, of which *Charlie Hebdo* had become a symbol, and that even prosecute independent journalists, was criticized by the human rights organization Reporters Without Borders as well as by *Charlie Hebdo* cartoonists.

What does all of this have to do with genuine societal discussion? And what can we learn from the *Charlie Hebdo* case for the Habermasian theory of deliberation?[2] After all, the identification many people showed with the victims and survivors of the attack ("Je suis Charlie") does not constitute an argumentative engagement in the strict sense. However, from a deliberative perspective such universal displays of solidarity should be valued as a precondition of more genuine discussion in the aftermath of the crisis. Mediated public rituals like the Republican March can promote inclusion across the divide between Muslims and non-Muslims and thus strengthen the social bonds necessary for camp-bridging deliberation (functions (2) and (3) in table 6.2). They might also mitigate the danger of hysterical reactions to the attacks through an experience of collective self-efficacy that helps overcome the state of shock, and might initiate public discussion about the reasons for, and new ways to prevent, such attacks in the future (function (6)). From a deliberative perspective it could also be hoped that the curtailment of civil rights often observed after threat crises like this might be kept open to later revision on the basis of that feeling of collective self-efficacy. In the case of France, this hope was frustrated, however, as the even more barbarous attacks in November 2015 and July 2016 resulted in a protracted state of emergency only partly lifted much later. The long-term trajectory of public debate is thus contingent on external

events and strategic action and cannot be foreseen or prede-
termined by public rituals.

Moreover, public rituals also carry certain dangers. In
the case of *Charlie Hebdo* public solidarity effectively meant
hailing a potentially divisive form of secularism that has very
particular roots in French political culture. *Charlie Hebdo* is
by no means a right-wing, racist publication, but its variant
of secularism (*laïcité*) is closely tied to anti-clericalism and
forcefully claims a right to be blasphemous. The surviving
Charlie Hebdo cartoonist Luz (Rénald Luzier) explains that it
has always been *Charlie*'s intention to break taboos and shat-
ter symbols, including the symbols of all three monotheistic
religions, Christianity, Judaism, and Islam.[3] Luz also wants
his cartoons to be "irresponsible" again, i.e. not responsible
for the reactions of people with a "different sense of humor."
On the occasion of the first anniversary of the attack, *Charlie
Hebdo* published a special issue on January 6, 2016. Its title
page shows God running away with blood on his caftan and
a machine gun on his back. The headline reads: "After one
year: The murderer is still on the run." *Charlie Hebdo* still
claims the right to blasphemy and therefore has become a
symbol of the unrestricted right to free expression and a
putative "right to offend."

From a deliberative perspective, this type of secularism –
and the mass identification with it through "Je suis
Charlie" – jeopardizes camp-bridging deliberation between
secular and religious groups. Habermas (2006b) grants a
positive role for religion in the public sphere because religion can serve as a source for moral intuitions not otherwise
accessible to a secular society, thereby enriching public discourse. Of course, Habermas would never condone any legal
restriction on the freedom of expression, but it is clear at the
same time that for genuine discussion to flourish it is beneficial to exercise that right with collective voluntary restraint.

How can deliberative theory help navigate this seeming contradiction? Two arguments are particularly important here, one hinting back at the role of satire for deliberation and the other one related to "meta-deliberation." First, *Charlie Hebdo* cartoons often point to problems in the way religion is practiced or instrumentalized. If made explicit, this normative problematization can at the same time be an important argumentative resource for public debate (functions (4) and (5) in table 6.2). Its potentially offensive form should not be an excuse to ignore its substance altogether. Second, however, such transfer of latent argumentation into the realm of explicit discussion should be accompanied by a healthy dose of meta-deliberation, i.e. explicit discussion about the context and the rules for public debate. To mitigate communicative escalation, it would be beneficial to explain and reflect on the version of secularism traditionally found in France and see it in relation to other, less militant types of secularism (Göle 2010) – rather than just celebrating French *laïcité* unequivocally. Apart from providing context, meta-deliberation has also helped in publicly reflecting on the rules of discussion by debating how freedom of expression and deliberative self-restraint can be balanced. A case in point here is the protest in May 2015 of some 200 PEN members against the conferral of the US PEN's "Freedom of Expression Courage award" to *Charlie Hebdo* (Schuessler 2015). Through such public debates meta-deliberation can be an important source of constant democratic innovation (Fung 2012), and it can generate a pluralistic deliberative system that allows for the collective contemplation about how, if necessary, religio-secular systems should be changed.

To sum up, the *Charlie Hebdo* case highlights the deliberative potential of mediated crises that lies in the opportunity to symbolically draw inclusive boundaries in defense of central values and to foster substantive, moderate debate across lines of deep difference. It is an empirical question to which degree what types of media in which kind of political discourse culture are positioned to successfully perform these normative functions. But the *Charlie Hebdo* case serves as a reminder that mediated public debate can seek truth and foster respect under certain conditions. Second, *Charlie Hebdo* shows that insisting on the right to free expression is not enough when it comes to creating healthy democratic contestation. Voluntary self-restraint is not tantamount to censorship or cowardice. Conversely, it is also not sufficient to insist on a putative "right not to be offended" if this means worshiping your own sensitivities and ignoring the argumentative kernel enclosed in provocative and even offensive criticism. At any rate, the *Charlie Hebdo* case is a potent reminder of the role that public demonstrations of solidarity and of camp-bridging unity can play in spawning respect and the willingness to listen.

SUMMARY

I have proposed a form of Habermas-inspired media analysis that systematically assesses the contributions of non-deliberative communication and media content to fostering genuine society-wide discussion. This directs our analytical attention to explicitly and transparently linking particular features of non-deliberative communication to specific elements of the macro-deliberative process. Implicit in this approach to non-deliberative media discourse is an understanding of deliberative democracy that is not restricted to narrow informational functions of the media or to the deployment of small-group deliberation forums throughout society. Deliberative democracy is instead seen as an experiment in large-scale debate and societal learning, at "intellectual and cultural innovation and producing and distributing new ideas and interpretations," as Bernhard Peters (2008c, 237) has said. A deliberative democracy does not produce true deliberative exchanges always and everywhere, but it has a special propensity to engender episodes of genuine public discussion and cultural innovation from time to time.

John Parkinson (2016) has brought a very similar point home with a colorful metaphor likening deliberative democracy to a clarinet.

> A B♭ clarinet is so called because its C is tuned to the absolute pitch of B♭ – the C on a clarinet is a tone lower than the C on a piano or a violin. Does that mean it can only play the note B♭? No. Does it mean it can only play in the key of B♭? No, of course not. But the tuning does give the instrument a particular timbre, a character that balances the brightness of a C tuning with the mellow depth of an A, something that has particular applications relative to other instruments in an ensemble. Clarinets, regardless of what they are tuned to, share a "woodwind" quality; oboes and bassoons have elements of that too but their twin reeds give them a, well, "reedy" quality that clarinets downplay. Trumpets and horns sound quite distinct relative to each other, but share the same brassiness compared with woodwinds and strings. [...] Music is not just about melodies, harmonies, tempo and rhythm – it is also about putting timbres together in sometimes-surprising ways. (Parkinson 2016, 15)

Parkinson goes on to suggest that the timbre of a deliberative democracy is not an additive quality attributable to a specific kind of forum or process. Instead deliberativeness ought to be understood as an emergent, summative quality of the entire democratic system. "To think of the deliberative quality as summative is to think of it as being produced by the scale and complexity of a given system, and not simply an ingredient which goes into a system" (Parkinson 2016, 17). This opens up the "possibility of a deliberative democracy in which none of its component parts meet all the criteria for deliberativeness but which expresses deliberativeness given a particular configuration of its constituent parts" (p. 17).

In my view, media discourse plays a decisive role in that configuration of democracy. The deliberativeness of a democratic system depends fundamentally on whether and how and to what degree media discourse from time to time facilitates genuine public discussion and learning. Against the backdrop of this more encompassing notion of the deliberative quality of democracy, my proposed form of media analysis neither marries nor divorces deliberation and non-deliberation. It does not propose that non-deliberative forms of communication are a natural and unproblematic component of deliberative exchanges. Nor does it propose that they are completely separate as some might prefer to see it, as if deliberation would have to be kept unpolluted by the toxins of non-deliberative forms of communication. I look instead at the more specific – and shifting – relations of both nurturing and abandonment between non-deliberative media discourse on the one hand and genuine societal debate as a macro-deliberative outcome on the other. In contrast to both marriage and divorce, I thus propose an "independent partnership" paradigm of Habermas-inspired media analysis in looking for the deliberative potentials of the wider forms of cultural production.

RECOMMENDED READING

Chambers, S. (2009) "Rhetoric and the public sphere: Has deliberative democracy abandoned mass democracy?" *Political Theory*, 37(3), pp. 323–50. doi: 10.1177/0090591709332336.

Parkinson, J. (2016) "On scholarly metaphors, or, what is deliberative about deliberative democracy?" Available at: https://ecpr.eu/Filestore/PaperProposal/90e7f4de-c707-447e-8a9a-7def01a57b73.pdf

Young, I. M. (2000) *Inclusion and democracy*. Oxford University Press, Oxford.

7

COUNTERPUBLICS AND THE ROLE

OF EMOTIONS

Habermas sees the deliberating publics of the eighteenth-century coffee houses, which he had theorized (and idealized) in his *Structural transformation of the public sphere* in 1962, reemerging on the Internet. "Internet communication on the World Wide Web seems to counterbalance the weaknesses associated with the anonymous and asymmetrical character of mass communication because it makes it possible to reintegrate interactive and deliberative elements into an unregulated exchange between partners who communicate with one another as equals, if only virtually" (Habermas 2009b, 157). But he then proceeds to grant salutary effects to the Internet only in authoritarian regimes where it helps undermine censorship and enables the formation of spontaneous public opinions. In democratic countries the mass audience of earlier times tends to disintegrate into a myriad of isolated online publics, according to Habermas. "The Web provides the hardware for the delocalization of an intensified and accelerated mode of communication, but it can itself do nothing to stem the centrifugal tendencies" (Habermas 2009b, 157f.).

Fragmentation is a hot issue in public sphere theory following Habermas. And it points to a more general question: How monolithic should the public sphere be conceptualized as being? And how do we account theoretically for relations between mainstream publics and "subaltern counterpublics" (Fraser 1992)? Counterpublics are collectives of speakers and listeners that are defined by their subjugation under, and their opposition to, a dominant or mainstream public. Counterpublics can develop elaborate communication infrastructures, both mediated and non-mediated, and can thus develop and "own" public spheres, which we may then call counterpublic spheres.

As we have seen in chapter 1, critics have pointed to Habermas's neglect of non-bourgeois public spheres: the plebeian or proletarian public sphere developing in the workplace and permeating public communication since the Industrial Revolution in eighteenth- and nineteenth-century Europe (Negt and Kluge 1972); or subcultural public spheres like the ones carved out of mainstream culture by, for example, the civil rights movement in the USA, the feminist movement, or the movement for homosexual emancipation (Breese 2011; Fraser 1992; Huspek 2007a; Squires 2002; Warner 2005). These counterpublic spheres are based on clearly identifiable collective entities, and the emergence of a public space of communication for these entities is dependent on their own emancipatory activity. Conversely, their success as movements depends on their ability to create public spaces of communication about their demands.

Habermas acknowledges these movements and the fact that they have created their own public spheres, but the thrust of his argument is about the inclusion of marginalized groups in an overarching "master" public sphere. How else is citizen communication to gain influence, even "communicative power," vis-à-vis the political power center, if not through the unifying process of focusing attention on just a few important issues and on developing recognizable opinions with enough clout to be reckoned with by politicians? To wield communicative power, the public sphere must be big, strong, and unitary so that political power-holders cannot afford to ignore its output, namely considered public opinion, for the sake of their own legitimation and, ultimately, their political survival. Habermas does not deny the existence of different layers and arenas in the public sphere, which he sees as a "highly complex network that branches out into a multitude of overlapping international, national, regional, local, and subcultural arenas" (Habermas 1996, 372). But the political functionality Habermas imagines for the public sphere directs his theoretical imagination to the aggregative and integrative processes needed to harness political influence. This has not remained uncontested.

SUBALTERN COUNTERPUBLICS

In her critique of the *Structural transformation of the public sphere* Fraser introduces the term "subaltern counterpublics" as "parallel discursive arenas where members of subordinated social groups invent and circulate counterdiscourses to formulate oppositional interpretations of their identities, interests, and needs" (Fraser 1992, 123). She argues that a multiplicity of publics is always preferable to a unitary public sphere and then analyzes their benefits in two idealtypes of societies: stratified societies with strong relations of domination and subordination between different groups (the USA is clearly Fraser's prototypical example here), and egalitarian, multicultural societies (for which no empirical prototype seems to exist). "[I]n stratified societies, subaltern counterpublics have a dual character. On the one hand, they function as spaces of withdrawal and regroupment; on the other hand, they also function as bases and training grounds for agitational activities directed toward wider publics" (Fraser 1992, 124). The "discursive relations among differentially empowered publics are as likely to take the form of contestation as that of deliberation" (p. 125).

But in Fraser's view, even in less conflictual, more egalitarian and culturally diverse societies a plurality of publics is preferable. "[P]ublic spheres are not only arenas for the formation of discursive opinion; in addition, they are arenas for the formation and enactment of social identities" (p. 125) that come with specific idioms and styles of expression. In order to allow everybody to participate in public communication on their own terms, these idioms and styles should be expressed in multiple public spheres as long as there is an additional overarching public sphere in which intercultural communication takes place. Thus, according to Fraser, counterpublics serve vital functions for the empowerment of subordinated groups vis-à-vis dominant groups, and participation in public communication is built on the right to use one's own expressive repertoire.

These ideas are taken up by Huspek (2007a; 2007b), who hinges the idea of the counterpublic on Habermas's concept of "systematically distorted communication," which we have encountered in chapter 2 (table 2.1). In systematically distorted communication "at least one of the parties is deceiving himself about the fact that he is acting with an attitude oriented to success and is only keeping up the appearance of communicative action" (Habermas 1984, 332). The root of systematically distorted communication can be psychopathological or ideological. Huspek maintains that members of the dominant public sphere ideologically deceive themselves about their tendency to keep perspectives from counterpublics silent in the mainstream arena and might at the same time be dismissive of counterpublic voices. And he rightly points out that Habermas does not offer much guidance on how systematically distorted communication can be practically overcome in real-world public discourse. To remedy this shortcoming, Huspek (2007b) recommends "rhetorical action" as a communication strategy for the subaltern counterpublic. In contrasting the mainstream *New York Times* with the voice of the African-American *New York Amsterdam News*, Huspek identifies and defends three types of counterpublic engagement that correspond to the three worlds which we inhabit as humans, i.e. the subjective, the objective, and the social world (Habermas 1984, 100).

• In relation to the subjective world Huspek (2007a) advocates uncivil forms of self-expression (e.g., calling the dominant other a "monster" or a "neo-fascist") that are directed not at silencing the dominant other, but at shaking them up (p. 834).
• With respect to the objective world Huspek condones what he calls "biased truth validity claims" to counter implicit biases in mainstream media coverage. These claims are "meant primarily to provoke spirited and informed debate" (Huspek 2007a, 835).
• And as regards the social world Huspek hails validity claims to moral rightness that irreverently challenge the existing political-legal order because it is fundamentally unjust, and that delegitimize the relations of dominance enshrined in it (Huspek 2007a, 838).

Habermas would presumably react to this proposal in a differentiated way. He has accepted uncivil speech and acts of civil disobedience as legitimate ways to garner attention for a cause, but he would certainly caution against any hopes of engendering genuine discussion by calling your opponent a "monster." With respect to biased truth claims, he would point out that in the public sphere truth claims are always made to support a particular position or perspective, but they can only be contested on the basis of contradicting facts. So "bias" is unavoidable, but also resolvable. Finally, the insertion of irreverent claims to moral rightness into extant discourses would be welcomed as it is exactly what drives social learning.

This argument serves to show that at least since *Between facts and norms* Habermas has developed a conception of the political public sphere that accommodates counterpublic tactics to the degree that they help engender genuine discussion on the societal macro level. Deviations from deliberative norms can indeed serve to remedy the intrusion of power into inter-public communication and help restore genuine discussion, as Estlund (2009, 194) has argued. Systematically distorted communication can best be dispelled by publicly exposing and criticizing the self-deception of the dominant speaker (that is, their unconscious rationalization of their dominant position) and relentlessly advancing rightness claims that make a better order imaginable to broader publics. And this can include uncivil tactics. The recent success of the "marriage equality" or "marriage for all" frame in a number of Western countries, resulting in the right for homosexuals to marry like heterosexuals, attests to the possibility of pushing back against systematically distorted communication and engendering large-scale social learning processes. Thus, inter-public contestation and even deliberation seem possible and promising from a Habermasian point of view. But what about the "formation and enactment of social identities" that Fraser (1992, 125) emphasizes as the second major function of public spheres?

ENACTING SOCIAL IDENTITIES IN PUBLIC DISCOURSE

This point has been argued most forcefully by Warner in his book *Publics and counterpublics* (2005). He does not look at public spheres in sociological terms, as a social space demarcated from other spheres by a particular logic. He looks at public spheres from a rhetorical angle, through the forms in which possible participants are addressed as members of a public that emerges exactly through these forms of address (Warner 2005, 67). In doing so Warner is able to detect the "self-fashioning" of public talk characterized by a tension between a pole of self-abstraction (exemplified by rational-critical discourse) and a pole of self-realization, that is, discourse of authentic expression.

According to Warner, the bourgeois model of the public sphere, which Habermas distills in his theory, marks the pole of self-abstraction. It entices speakers to talk as if they were talking not for themselves but for everybody. They (inadvertently) universalize their partial positions by pretending that the realization of their interests is in the public interest. Through this disembodied form of speech, public discourse renders the real persons speaking with their unmistakable identities, bodies, and desires invisible (Warner 1992, 382).

Counterpublics are not just groups of "subalterns with a reform program" (Warner 2005, 119). They differ radically in their preferred form of self-expression. The conflict between a counterpublic and the dominant public

> extends not just to ideas or policy questions but to the speech genres and modes of address that constitute the public or to the hierarchy among media. The discourse that constitutes it is not merely a different or alternative idiom

but one that in other contexts would be regarded with hostility or with a sense of indecorousness. [...] Friction against the dominant public forces the poetic-expressive character of counterpublic discourse to become salient in consciousness. (Warner 2005, 120)

In Warner's analysis, counterpublics self-constitute through their particular forms of "poetic world making" (2005, 114), which at the pole of self-realization comprise the particular ways of showing the body rather than only expressing thoughts. This creative-expressive dimension of counterpublics is especially difficult to accommodate in Habermas's perspective, particularly because it does not correspond to familiar forms of agency. Warner makes this point by juxtaposing the verbs that are usually associated with a public engaged in rational-critical discourse with those verbs that might characterize a queer counterpublic:

> All of the verbs for public agency are verbs for private reading, transposed upward to the aggregate of readers. Readers may scrutinize, ask, reject, opine, decide, judge, and so on. Publics can do exactly these things. And nothing else. [...] A queer public sphere might be one that throws shade, prances, disses, acts up, carries on, longs, fantasizes, throws fits, mourns, "reads." To take such attributions of public agency seriously, however, we would need to inhabit a culture with a different language ideology, a different social imaginary. (Warner 2005, 123f.)

In particular, it would be an imaginary that does not pit publics against the state, as Habermas does. "This is one of the things that happens when alternative publics are said to be social movements: they acquire agency in relation to the state. [...] For many counterpublics, to do so is to cede the original hope of transforming not just policy but the space of public life itself" (Warner 2005, 124).

For Habermas, transforming the space of public life through authentic self-expression has not been the center of interest. In his view, discourse in the public sphere is rooted in but, crucially, not identical to the lifeworld. Habermas (1996, 369) does emphasize that public communication has not only a manifest content (that is, Warner's "reform program") but also a "performative meaning." This meaning lies in actualizing the "function of an undistorted political public sphere as such" (Habermas 1996, 369). Following Cohen and Arato, Habermas contends that social movements "attempt to maintain existing structures of association and public influence, to generate subcultural counterpublics and counterinstitutions, to consolidate new collective identities, and to win new terrain in the form of expanded rights and reformed institutions" (p. 370). But the subcultural counterpublics mentioned here are conceptualized as idea-generators for public debate. Their capacity to produce creative self-expressions is registered, but Habermas's account aims at something else: To acquire collective meaning and political effectiveness, self-expression should ultimately yield *criticizable* ideas and positions whose validity claims to truth and moral rightness can, at least in principle, be problematized and discussed.

AFFECTIVE PUBLICS

One prominent, recent alternative to interpreting counterpublics as elements in a deliberative system is the idea of "affective publics" developed by Papacharissi (2015). She defines affective publics as "networked public formations that are mobilized and connected or disconnected through expressions of sentiment" (p. 125). Important examples include the Twitter activities of the Arab Spring movements (using the hashtag #egypt, for example) as well as the Occupy Wall Street protests (e.g., #ows) and their offspring in other parts of the world. Papacharissi shows how these "[a]ffective publics are powered by affective statements of opinion, fact, or a blend of both, which in turn produce ambient, always-on feeds that further connect and pluralize expression in regimes democratic and otherwise" (p. 129).

Her interest is not in the deliberative quality of such expressions; in fact, she explicitly warns against what she sees as "retrofitting [the Internet] into models of civic engagement that speak to the political economies of prior eras" (p. 26). Papacharissi sees the civic potential of the Internet in its potential to unleash its users' affect and facilitate "affective attunement" between them in a constant stream of networked communication.

> Media typically invite audiences to consume content via affective relationships developed with particular media genres and media personas. These affective relationships may lead to the emergence and cultivation of particular feelings and emotions, but it is essential not to confuse affect with emotion and feeling. While affect contains a particular energy, mood, or movement that may lead to particular feeling, and possibly the subsequent expression of emotion, it both precedes and sustains or possibly annuls feeling and emotion. (Papacharissi 2015, 21)

Affect is a force that lies behind or beneath overt expressions of emotions like anger, joy, or compassion – as well as overt expressions of thoughts and reasoning. "It is the intensity with which we experience both reason and emotion" (p. 134). As such, affect creates the "texture" of political expression, not its content (p. 118). This, in turn, means that affective publics can be progressive or conservative, they can be radical on the left as well as on the right wing of the political spectrum.

> Over time, affect may lead to subtle disruptions of power hierarchies, which cumulatively may produce considerable energies of resistance and renegotiation of boundaries. At the same time, affect may also dominate expression and distract from factuality, as is the case with the affective structures that support the growth of the Tea Party movement in the United States. Affective mechanisms increase awareness of an issue and in so doing amplify the intensity of that awareness. They do not inherently enhance understanding of a problem, deepen one's knowledge on a particular issue, or lead to thick forms of civic engagement with public affairs. (p. 120)

The contingent political nature of affective publics is highlighted by Karpf (2017) in his creative attempt to imagine what a second edition of Papacharissi's book might look like that takes the presidency of Donald Trump in the USA into account. The pre-Trump movements Papacharissi analyzes, Karpf writes, "appear noteworthy for their earnestness" (p. 292). The 2016 election, however, has seen the massive deployment of online trolling and political bots, that is, computer programs that automatically create social media messages to support one candidate and denigrate the other. Both the Trump and Clinton campaigns have used political bots, but they were much more massive on Trump's side, including the "alt-right" movement that backed him (Woolley and Guilbeault 2017). "[I]t seems almost as if Trump's supporters on social media developed a sort of weaponized, automated affective public" (Karpf 2017, 202). Through trolling and botnets, affective intensity was not only strategically but also deceptively fabricated, and it goes without saying that weaponized affective publics are deeply problematic not only from a deliberative point of view, but also from almost any other democratic theory. Even agonistic conceptions, which favor robust exchanges of values, as we have seen in chapter 4, build their argument on the presumption of *authentic* political self-expression.

In addition to the fabricated nature of some social media-based affective publics, there is a larger discussion about the relation between emotion and reason that emerges from Papacharissi's account (see also Wahl-Jorgensen 2013).

> Popular discourses about normative forms of civic engagement frequently set emotion against reason and feeling against thought. Thus, certain forms of civic engagement are termed inadequate for being too emotional and lacking rational foundation while others are termed too logical and stripped of emotional engagement. And yet logic and emotion can and do co-exist. In quintessential Spinozian terms, logic helps interpret emotion and emotion gives meaning to logic. (Papacharissi 2015, 134)

It is this complementary and conjunctural nature of emotion and reason that actually helps to reconnect – despite Papacharissi's clear rejection of the idea – the concept of affective publics to a deliberative outlook on civic engagement in networked public spheres. Affective attunement and the expression of emotions are by no means *per se* problematic or unproblematic. Instead, a deliberative perspective would always ask: *Which kinds* of emotions are being expressed and affectively intensified in public discourse, and *what functions* do they perform in relation to genuine public discussion? Two strands of deliberative theorizing can be distinguished here. One focuses on the potential benefits of empathy for engendering truly open discussion, learning, and, it is hoped, solidarity. The other one looks at emotions as affective reactions to moral violations or disagreements and assesses their functions in the moral justification of actions. In the remainder of this chapter I will turn to each strand in turn.

EMPATHY AND DELIBERATION

Several scholars have suggested that empathy fosters genuine, open debate because being empathetic opens ourselves to the concerns of others (Morrell 2010; Wahl-Jorgensen 2013; Scudder 2016). It is important to note that empathy is not a discrete emotion, but the capacity to feel like others might feel (affective empathy) or to understand their feelings and perspectives (cognitive empathy). Affective empathy can be deployed with different kinds of emotions, be they positive or negative. We can be empathetic with other people's sadness or with their joy. Cognitive empathy, in turn, is key to deliberation, which is, after all, about reciprocal role-taking in an attempt to understand the other's perspective (Neblo 2003, 8; see also Morrell 2010). The affective side of empathy – preferably in conjunction with an element of genuine curiosity – seems like a most potent emotional base for facilitating and giving meaning to that cognitive role-taking and thus for truly open discussion. Therefore, empathy can be connected to learning about others and from others. In addition, affective empathy might also motivate acts of solidarity with people experiencing hardship.

However, empathy's role in deliberative theory has also been questioned. Scudder (2016) warns that, because empathy is based on imagination of the feelings of others, it might lead us to project such imagined feelings onto them rather than reflecting or doubling their feelings and perspectives in our experience. According to Scudder, empathy is ill-suited as a deliberative ideal because it undermines actual listening practices between people. She aims instead at safeguarding *democratic listening* against merely imagining what others might feel and think. Scudder (2016, 538) also argues that "successful appeals to empathy often implicitly rely on shared conceptions of the good, which cannot be assumed in the deliberative framework." And indeed, as we have seen in chapter 4, Habermas argues against the "ethical overload" of the republican conception of democracy, that is, an unrealistic presumption of shared values that tends to constrict public discourse to a particular community of value, rather than to everybody affected by an issue.

The strength of Scudder's account lies in reminding us that empathy's benefits unfold best in actual communication rather than in merely internal feeling or thinking, which are indeed prone to the dangers of projection. Empathy alone is certainly not a sufficient ideal for deliberative democracy. But empathic concern can be tested against the feelings and thoughts of others in actual communicative exchanges, in which both the sources and targets of empathy simultaneously gain voice and listen. And thus the benefits of empathy can be preserved for democracy if mass and network media organize debates in which various actors both speak and listen to what others have to say. Facilitating communicatively tested empathy thus seems like a formidable task for deliberatively minded media theorists and practitioners.

In an even broader perspective, empathic concern for others can also be connected to what psychologists call self-transcendent emotions. "[S]elf-transcendent emotions are other-oriented, diminishing one's focus on the self and encouraging greater sensitivity and attunement to others" (Stellar et al. 2017, 2). Important examples of self-transcendent emotions are not only *compassion* (connected to pity, sympathy, and, yes, empathic concern), but also *gratitude* (connected to appreciation) and *awe* (related to admiration, inspiration, and elevation) (see Habermas 1998, 4f.). It is intuitively plausible that deliberation is deeply connected to transcending the self because it involves listening to the needs and reasons of others. So, self-transcendent emotions like compassion, gratitude, and awe will have to play an important role in an emergent deliberative conception of emotions. They might shift the tone of mediated debate away from self-interest. Consider the example of media coverage of the European refugee situation in 2015/16. Mediated debate that at least partly features compassion for the refugees' fate, that gives voice to refugees' own gratitude toward the welcoming nations (as well as to their grievances), and that maybe even shows admiration for their bravery in fleeing will likely be a supportive context for positions and arguments that favor an open refugee policy. Exploring the connections between specific self-transcendent emotions and particular positions and arguments expressed in mediated debates seems like a highly fruitful route for future Habermasian media analysis.

But a nascent deliberative theory of emotions might not even stop there. Some of the positive self-centered emotions also seem to be connected to an opening of discursive space and an expansion of the publicly available argument repertoire. The emotion of amazement, for one, might open up debate in this way, if we think about unexpected positive turns of events like the fall of the Berlin Wall in November 1989, for example. The same might be true for hope, an anticipation that the societal conditions being discussed can (be made to) change for the better, for example in imminent pre-revolutionary situations like the beginning of the Arab Spring. Amazement and hope might thus mark an acceleration of the societal learning process that lies at the center, as we have seen in chapter 6, of the deliberative perspective on democracy.

MORAL EMOTIONS AS JUSTIFICATIONS

Habermas approaches emotions from a slightly different angle, not through the role-taking aspect of deliberation enshrined in communicatively tested empathy, but through the emotional underpinnings of moral judgment. He looks at emotions as affective reactions in situations of moral violation or disagreement and finds that they perform an important function in morally justifying individual and collective action. "Feelings seem to have a similar function for the moral justification of action as sense perceptions have for the theoretical justification of facts" (Habermas 1990, 50). As Neblo (2003, 3) aptly observed:

> If we stop and think about where science would be without recourse to sense perception, it becomes obvious that it is decisively false to claim that Habermas's discourse theory makes no room for the emotions, or even that they play a marginal role. Whatever one thinks of the ultimate adequacy of his formulation, it creates an enormous and absolutely essential role for affective intelligence in his theoretical system.

For Habermas, the natural place for emotions is in what he has called practical discourse. As we have seen in chapter 2, in practical discourse validity claims to moral rightness are problematized, and thus contradictory moral judgments are exchanged. Such judgments often have an emotional quality, which is less salient in theoretical discourse where truth claims are discussed.

When we examine moral disagreements, we must include affective reactions in the class of moral utterances. [...] The critical and self-critical stances we adopt toward transgressions find expression in affective attitudes: from the third person perspective, in abhorrence, indignation, and contempt, from the perspective of those affected, in feelings of violation or resentment towards second persons, and from the first person perspective, in shame and guilt. (Habermas 1998, 4f.)

In situations of perceived moral transgression the full array of negative emotions mentioned by Habermas in the third-person perspective – abhorrence, indignation, contempt – serves to create attention and urgency. For example, Brady et al. (2017) show that moral-emotional words in messages on social media will boost their diffusion throughout the network, with every additional moral-emotional word in a tweet increasing the retweet rate by 20 percent on average. Moral urgency can of course also be created when those affected by a moral transgression against themselves (second-person perspective) publicly express their feelings of violation and resentment. This is equivalent to the expression of "feelings of injustice" that Garcez and Maia (2014) have studied in social media. By comparison, public admissions of shame and guilt as affective reactions from the first-person perspective of the perpetrator are less likely in mediated debates. Still, an exchange in which participants were able to see their own failings could lead to a somewhat more open discussion climate afterward. Think about German Chancellor Willy Brandt's highly mediated kneeling in front of the memorial for the victims of the Warsaw

Ghetto in 1970 – a public gesture of humility and penance that seems to have thoroughly changed German–Polish relations and Germany's public image worldwide, even though Brandt was not a perpetrator himself, but acted as the representative of the perpetrator nation.

According to Habermas, moral feelings – whether publicly expressed by perpetrators, victims, or onlookers of moral transgression – do not just stand for themselves but serve as justifications in practical discourse. "Because they express implicit judgments, these feelings in which actors express their pro and con attitudes are correlated with evaluations. [...] The claim that moral judgments admit of justification also reveals itself in these moral feelings and evaluations, for they differ from other feelings and evaluations in being tied to obligations that function as reasons" (Habermas 1998, 4f.). The expression of moral feelings thus helps sustain a social fabric in which moral obligations are communicated and discussed. Of course, moral judgments and obligations will often be contested in mediated debates. Consequently, different moral feelings will clash. But practical discourse exists exactly to problematize and debate moral claims, including moral feelings – a process in which not every moral claim will come out as equally legitimate.

From a Habermasian perspective it is thus not enough for counterpublic actors to voice moral feelings of indignation and contempt at what they perceive as moral transgression, even if they manage to secure a counterpublic space for themselves or a strong voice in the dominant public sphere. The legitimacy of the claim matters, too, and it hinges on the degree to which the claim can be backed by good arguments that the feeling of indignation or violation reacts to actual injustice. This is why right-wing counterpublics such as anti-immigrant networks in Europe or the "alt-right" movement in the United States cannot be considered subaltern counterpublics. They do not express the injustice experienced by subordinated social groups, but by and large aim at maintaining structures of domination and exclusion. Therefore, from a deliberative perspective, these counterpublics may be structurally similar to those tied to subordinated social groups (see Töpfl and Piwoni 2015), but they are less deliberatively beneficial and less democratically legitimate. To empirically tease out this difference in legitimacy of different expressions of moral feelings in mediated discussions is another important task for future Habermasian media analysis.

SUMMARY

The existence of rebellious counterpublics has been leveled against Habermas's conceptions of the public sphere and deliberative democracy in at least two tightly connected ways. First, counterpublics have been said to make a unitary understanding of "the" public sphere obsolete. Counterpublics demand their own discursive spaces for internal identity enactment and strategy development, and as such are said to expose and debunk the hegemonic or repressive character of a unitary master sphere. This push against the unitary is often coupled with an attack on civility and argumentative exchange as a normative criterion for public communication. Demanding civil speech in a hierarchical and competitive discourse situation then seems like just another tool of oppression. Consequently, affective and uncivil forms of authentic expression are not only hailed but also pitched against Habermas.

I have approached these twin attacks by pointing to lesser-known strands in Habermas-inspired theorizing and research. Concerning the civility criterion I have pointed to the fact that Habermas does accommodate counterpublic tactics for gaining attention and creating urgency. But instead of theoretically pitching emotionally charged, affective publics against genuine public discussion, I have tried to use Habermas's scattered remarks on emotions and the emerging debate on empathy to sketch the role of emotions in mediated public discussion. Habermas does not conceptualize public debate as disembodied, self-abstracted speech in ideal speech situations. Instead, his writings allow for more systematic research into the emotions underlying public discussion by directing analytical attention particularly to situations of moral disagreement as a source of emotional engagement.

But emotional engagement alone is not enough. A deliberative conception of emotions hinges on the legitimacy of the moral claims, including the moral feelings expressed in mediated debate. By tying emotional expression to practical discourse in this way, Habermasian theory provides a yardstick for this legitimacy, namely that moral indignation is backed by good reasons, not just by social power or the sheer energy of the affect. Most extreme right-wing, and probably also some extreme left-wing, counterpublics would not pass this "deliberative benefit" test.

Finally, not only negative but also positive emotions can play a role in engendering genuine public discussion and facilitating collective learning. As I have tried to show, empathic concern, if tested for validity in actual communicative exchanges with its addressees, can open discussions up to the concerns of formerly neglected others. More generally, positive self-transcendent emotions like compassion, gratitude, and awe are likely to have distinct relations to particular argument repertoires and may thus generate more open and inclusive mediated debates. And even amazement and hope can be beneficial, as they may mark moments of acceleration in the large-scale learning process that lies at the heart of the deliberative project.

RECOMMENDED READING

Neblo, M. A. (2003) "Impassioned democracy: The role of emotion in deliberative theory." Unpublished manuscript. Available at: https://polisci.osu.edu/sites/polisci.osu.edu/files/NebloImpassioned4Web_0.pdf

Stellar, J. E., Gordon, A. M., Piff, P. K., Cordaro, D., Anderson, C. L., Bai, Y., Maruskin, L. A., and Keltner, D. (2017) "Self-transcendent emotions and their social functions: Compassion, gratitude, and awe bind us to others through prosociality," *Emotion Review*, 9(3), pp. 1–8. doi: 10.1177/1754073916684557.

Wahl-Jorgensen, K. (2013) "Future directions for political communication scholarship: Considering emotion in mediated public participation." In: Valdivia, A. N. (ed.) *The international encyclopedia of media studies*. Wiley-Blackwell, Hoboken, NJ, pp. 455–77.

CONCLUSION

Some authors in media and communication studies refer to Jürgen Habermas's work in very scant form. A fleeting reference to "Habermas 1989" coupled with a disparaging remark according to which his concept of the bourgeois public sphere obviously fails to capture the complexities of contemporary public spheres – and off the author goes to other matters, other authors, seemingly better ideas. In such superficial invocations Habermas is in danger of becoming a straw man. Of course, one could apologetically claim that this is the price to be paid for the admirably wide reception and powerful impact that Habermas's work has enjoyed in communication scholarship and other disciplines. But this is a lame excuse for several reasons.

For one, "Habermas 1989" – his *Structural transformation of the public sphere* – is only one of Habermas's central works relevant to media and communication scholarship, and his earliest and least developed one at that, published in German in 1962. His magnum opus, *The theory of communicative action* (Habermas 1984/1987b), remains a hidden treasure for all but the most dedicated readers in media and communication studies. Not all communication scholars have read the very pertinent chapter 8 of *Between facts and norms* (1996) on the role of civil society and the political public sphere in a deliberative democracy. And although many in the field have listened to Habermas's keynote address at the annual conference of the International Communication Association held in Dresden, Germany, in June 2006 (Habermas 2006a), few know the much-elaborated 50-page version of that keynote published three years later (Habermas 2009b).

I am citing the stages of Habermas's theoretical engagement with the media here again to show how his thinking about the media has evolved in significant and productive ways, including an engagement with the notorious complexities of contemporary public spheres. In conclusion, I would like to summarize what I see as Habermas's strengths in theorizing media and communication as well as some limitations and points of departure for extensions and revisions.

An obvious strength, in my view, is the fact that Habermas looks at media and communication from a distinct and well-developed critical-normative perspective. This helps us as a discipline to preserve a critical distance from our objects of study even though and while many students in the field train to become media and communication experts who will work in the industries so critically analyzed. More particularly, however, Habermas's critical-normative standard provides us with the means to assess

• whether mediated political communication is an instance of genuine bottom-up democratic engagement or an instance of top-down domination, and

• whether the opinions developed in public communication
are well considered or uninformed, whether they constitute well-founded judgments or mere prejudice.

This is a most welcome reminder in a day and age in which
"post-factual" and "post-truth" democracy have become
buzzwords. In wrestling with both conscious deception
in public communication and unconscious beliefs in the
"truthiness" of unproven allegations, a second strength of
Habermas's theoretical work comes to the fore. His systematic analysis of the sources of rationality in mediated and
non-mediated communication helps us distinguish what
the ubiquitous conflicts and debates are actually about. It
makes a big difference both for researchers and for citizens
to know whether disagreement is about truth claims, claims
to moral rightness, or claims to sincerity or truthfulness. As
Habermas has demonstrated, the first two can be argued in
public debate, whereas the problem of insincere, unauthen-
tic, or deceptive communication must be tackled by deeper
structural changes to the communication system and more
long-term observation of the democratic performance of
speakers in the public sphere.

This leads me to a third strength. Habermas situates
media debates in a comprehensive, yet specific model of
the democratic process that sets itself apart from its rivals
by its focus on collective learning. The model of deliberative democracy, which has spawned an enormously
productive theoretical and empirical literature, reminds us
that mediated public debates should not just ritually recy-
cle long-held beliefs, but incubate new ideas. Democracy
is not only a mechanism to aggregate interests and
produce collectively binding decisions but also a large-
scale experiment in collective learning and intellectual
innovation.

Turning to some limitations in Habermas's theory of the media, it seems to me that precisely this open-ended learning process is to some degree lost or underrated in Habermas's most recent models of the media's role in political communication (Habermas 2009b; see chapter 3 of this book). In those models, the mass media are granted quite circumscribed functional roles that basically amount to transmitting all available information and the resulting decision options related to particular policy proposals to the citizens through published opinions. While this is a highly important core function of mediated communication, it does seem to constrain the role of media debate to preparing political deliberations and decisions that are then taking place elsewhere. Beyond the obvious fact that Habermas has not provided to date a thorough analysis of the Internet, this functionally restricted view of the mass media underrates the culture-producing capacities of all communication media.

As surprising as it may seem, it turns out that since the 1990s Habermas does not appear to be interested in "the media" that much anymore. To be more precise, he is less interested in the cultural roots of mediated public spheres, both in a critical and in a descriptive sense, than one might expect. This marks a clear contrast to his keen interest in the cultural roots of the early bourgeois public sphere in *Structural transformation of the public sphere* (see chapter 1) and defies the fact that "culture" features as one of the three essential pillars of the lifeworld in his *Theory of communicative action* (chapter 2). In Habermas's more recent writings, many of the phenomena that scholars of media and communication are interested in do not feature prominently:

- the cultural contexts of media production (including non-Western cultures),

- the cultural resources used for mediated engagement, and
- the creation processes and meaning patterns in contemporary media of all kinds.

Habermas-inspired media analysts would be well advised to tap into the lesser-known parts of the theory of communicative action more deeply, in order both to ground mediated public discussion in the wider context of cultural production and meaning-making in the lifeworld, and to understand the full plurality of media, communities, and participants in contemporary mediated public spheres. Based on this reading of his work, I see three complementary routes for empirical research using and extending Habermas's theory of media, public spheres, and deliberative democracy. These routes roughly correspond to the themes I have explored in chapters 5, 6, and 7, respectively.

Route 1: Applying deliberative standards: The first, most traditional option is to apply Habermas's concept of deliberation to comparatively assess degrees of deliberativeness in different types of media content as well as study their structural and cultural preconditions and consequences. Since the early 2000s we have seen quite a wave of studies looking at the deliberative qualities of various media types and formats, including online deliberation, and there is not so much more to be gained here. But the systematic study of those structural conditions under which deliberative performance flourishes or wanes is still in its early stages and should be extended. Even more in need of elaboration are studies pinpointing individual and societal consequences of higher or lower levels of deliberative media output. Are countries with more deliberative media system outputs also characterized by higher levels of collective learning and/or civic solidarity, as Habermas's approach would suggest? This line of research would crucially include an exploration of what deliberative media content means for citizens' ability to *listen* to their fellow citizens even across deep divides (see Bassel 2017), in addition to the much-researched question of how citizens acquire voice. After all, democratic listening is a hallmark of the deliberative model of democracy and sets Habermas-inspired media analysis apart from its conceptual rivals.

Route 2: Culturally embedding deliberation: The second possibility for Habermas-inspired media analysis lies in studying public deliberation as embedded in mediated contestation more broadly conceived, including rhetoric, narrative, satire, protest, and public ritual in both their textual and visual modes of presentation. In chapter 6 I have developed a proposal to assess the contributions that these various non-deliberative forms of communication and media discourse can make to fostering genuine societal discussion and learning. This "embedding" strategy connects Habermas's more recent elaboration of deliberative communication back to his analysis of the structures of the lifeworld, and engages in a kind of cultural re-appropriation of deliberation. In making that proposal I distance myself from those who call for an analysis of media or culture "beyond" or "against" rational-critical discussion. The value of Habermas's theory for communication and media research lies precisely in facilitating a focus on the cultural embeddedness of deliberation that avoids the limitations not only (a) of analyzing deliberation as a formal procedure isolated from its real-world cultural context, but also (b) of analyzing media culture in isolation from (or juxtaposition with) the formation of well-considered opinions and collective learning. Bernhard Peters's (2008b; 2008c) explorations of how public debate is constrained by specific traditions of "public culture" – characterized by a set of idea-generating actors and institutions and distinct collective interpretations and self-understandings – lead the way to a culturally embedded public sphere analysis.

Route 3: Anchoring deliberation in emotion: The third route, which I have sketched in chapter 7, strays even further from the beaten paths of Habermasian media analysis. It aims at uncovering the roots of emotions in Habermas's theory, particularly in moral judgment and practical discourse, and at systematically exploring how reason is anchored in and complemented by emotion in mediated public discussion. Hasty readers of Habermas's work might not realize what Neblo (2003, 1) has put so succinctly: "For a deliberative democrat, the antonym of reason is not emotion, but rather power." Emotions can help unravel illegitimate power. But it is vital to ask: Which emotions, propelled by which kinds of (affective) publics, intertwined with which types of rational arguments, and in which types of mediated public debates, can unravel illegitimate power? I suspect that answers to this question will lead to an understanding of mediated public exchanges that is deeper, more critically discerning, and truer to life. Both negative moral emotions and positive self-transcending emotions are prime candidates for uncovering the affective underpinnings of genuine mediated discussions.

The overarching goal for all three routes toward future research lies in developing a normatively guided, culturally sensitive, and richly contextualized analysis of mediated discussions as instances of democratic contestation. An analysis like this would also open the window on how mediated communication can contribute to the gradual disentangling of those wicked, intractable problems with which global society is confronted. It would help identify the entry points for conflict resolution in polarized democracies and between entrenched enemies (see Steiner et al. 2017). I hope to have shown that Habermas's work continues to be an open quarry, a breeding ground, and at times a guidebook for exactly this type of inquiry.

NOTES

Chapter 4 Mediated Public Spheres
1 The following paragraph is based on passages from Wessler, Rinke, and Löb (2016).

Chapter 5 Deliberative Qualities Of News And Discussion Media
1 The following paragraphs are partly based on Wessler and Rinke (2014, 4–5).

Chapter 6 Non-Deliberative Media Discourse
1 "Wenn einer bei uns einen guten Witz macht, dann sitzt halb Deutschland auf dem Sofa und nimmt übel" (Wrobel 1919; my translation).
2 The following paragraphs are partly based on Wessler, Rinke, and Löb (2016).
3 Interview with *VICE News* on January 31, 2015; accessed on YouTube.

REFERENCES

Adorno, T. W. and Horkheimer, M. (2002) *Dialectic of enlightenment*. Stanford University Press, Stanford.

Althaus, S. L. (2012) "What's good and bad in political communication research? Normative standards for evaluating media and citizen performance." In: Semetko, H. A. and Scammell, M. (eds.) *Sage Handbook of Political Communication*. SAGE, Thousand Oaks, CA, pp. 97–145.

Ausserhofer, J. and Maireder, A. (2013) "National politics on Twitter: Structures and topics of a networked public sphere," *Information, Communication & Society*, 16(3), pp. 291–314. doi: 10.1080/1369118X.2012.756050.

Baker, C. E. (2002) *Media, markets, and democracy*. Cambridge University Press, Cambridge.

Bassel, L. (2017). *The politics of listening: Possibilities and challenges for democratic life*. Palgrave Pivot, London.

Bennett, L. W. (2007) "Relief in hard times: A defense of Jon Stewart's comedy in an age of cynicism," *Critical*

Studies in Media Communication, 24(3), pp. 278–83. doi: 10.1080/07393180701521072.

Bennett, W. L., Pickard, V. W., Iozzi, D. P., Schroeder, C. L., Lagos, T., and Evans Caswell, C. (2004) "Managing the public sphere: Journalistic construction of the great globalization debate," *Journal of Communication*, 54(3), pp. 437–55. doi: 10.1093/joc/54.3.437.

Bennett, W. L. and Segerberg, A. (2013) "The logic of connective action: Digital media and the personalization of contentious politics," *Information, Communication & Society*, 15(5), pp. 739–768. doi: 10.1080/1369118X.2012.670661.

Benson, R. (2009) "Shaping the public sphere: Habermas and beyond," *The American Sociologist*, 40, pp. 175–92. doi: 10.1007/s12108-009-9071-4.

Benson, R. (2013) *Shaping immigration news: A French–American comparison*. Cambridge University Press, Cambridge.

Bohman, J. (1996) *Public deliberation: Pluralism, complexity, and democracy*. MIT Press, Cambridge, MA.

Boswell, J. (2013) "Why and how narrative matters in deliberative systems," *Political Studies*, 61(3), pp. 620–36. doi: 10.1111/j.1467-9248.2012.00987.x.

Brady, W. J., Wills, J. A., Jost, J. T., Tucker, J. A., and Van Bavel, J. J. (2017) "Emotion shapes the diffusion of moralized content in social networks," *Proceedings of the National Academy of Sciences of the United States of America*, 114(28), pp. 7313–18. doi: 10.1073/pnas.1618923114.

Breese, B. E. (2011) "Mapping the variety of public spheres," *Communication Theory*, 21(2), pp. 130–49.

Brüggemann, M. and Wessler, H. (2014) "Transnational communication as deliberation, ritual and strategy," *Communication Theory*, 24(4), pp. 394–414.

Buckels, E. E., Trapnell, P. D., and Paulhus, D. L. (2014) "Trolls just want to have fun," *Personality and Individual Differences*, 67, pp. 97–102. doi: 10.1016/j.paid.2014.01.016.

Burkart, R. and Lang, A. (2007) "Die Theorie des kommunikativen Handelns von Jürgen Habermas: Eine kommentierte Textcollage." In: Burkart, R. and Hömberg, R. (eds.) *Kommunikationstheorien: Ein Textbuch zur Einführung*. Wilhelm Braumüller, Vienna, pp. 42–71.

Calhoun, C. (ed.) (1992) *Habermas and the public sphere*. MIT Press, Cambridge, MA.

Chambers, S. (2009) "Rhetoric and the public sphere: Has deliberative democracy abandoned mass democracy?" *Political Theory*, 37(3), pp. 323–50. doi: 10.1177/0090591709332336.

Chambers, S. (2010) "Theories of political justification," *Philosophy Compass*, 5(11), pp. 893–903. doi: 10.1111/j.1747-9991.2010.00344.x.

Cinalli, M. and O'Flynn, I. (2014) "Public deliberation, network analysis and the political integration of Muslims in Britain," *The British Journal of Politics and International Relations*, 16(3), pp. 428–51. doi: 10.1111/1467-856X.12003.

Dahlberg, L. (2001) "The Internet and democratic discourse: Exploring the prospects of online deliberative forums extending the public sphere," *Information, Communication & Society*, 4(4), pp. 615–33. doi: 10.1080/13691180110097030.

Dahlberg, L. (2011) "Re-constructing digital democracy: An outline of four 'positions'," *New Media & Society*, 13(6), pp. 855–72. doi: 10.1177/1461444810389569.

Dahlberg, L. (2014) "The Habermasian public sphere and exclusion: An engagement with poststructuralist-influenced critics," *Communication Theory*, 24(1), pp. 21–41. doi: 10.1111/comt.12010.

Dayan, D. and Katz, E. (1992) *Media events: The live broadcasting of history*. Harvard University Press, Cambridge, MA.

Dryzek, J. S. (2005) "Deliberative democracy in divided societies: Alternatives to agonism and analgesia," *Political Theory*, 33(2), pp. 218–42.

Dryzek, J. S. (2009) "Democratization as deliberative capacity building," *Comparative Political Studies*, 42(11), pp. 1379–1402. doi: 10.1177/0010414009332129.

Eckert, S., Chadha, K., and Koliska, M. (2014) "Stuck in first gear: The case of the German political 'blogosphere'," *International Journal of Communication*, 8(1), pp. 626–45.

Erman, E. (2009) "What is wrong with agonistic pluralism? Reflections on conflict in democratic theory," *Philosophy & Social Criticism*, 35(9), pp. 1039–62. doi: 10.1177/0191453709343385.

Estlund, D. M. (2009) *Democratic authority: A philosophical framework*. Princeton University Press, Princeton, NJ.

Etling, B., Faris, R., Palfrey, J., Gasser, U., Kelly, J., and Alexanyan, K. (2010a) *Public discourse in the Russian blogosphere: Mapping RuNet politics and mobilization*. Berkman Center Research Publication no. 2010–11.

Etling, B., Kelly, J., Faris, R., and Palfrey, J. (2010b) "Mapping the Arabic blogosphere: Politics and dissent online," *New Media & Society*, 12(8), pp. 1225–43. doi: 10.1177/1461444810385096.

Ettema, J. S. (2007) "Journalism as reason-giving: Deliberative democracy, institutional accountability, and the news media's mission," *Political Communication*, 24(2), pp. 143–60.

Evans, S. K., Pearce, K. E., Vitak, J., and Treem, J. (2016) "Explicating affordances: A conceptual framework for understanding affordances in communication research," *Journal of Computer-Mediated Communication*, 22(1), pp. 35–52. doi: 10.1111/jcc4.12180.

Ferree, M. M., Gamson, W. A., Gerhards, J., and Rucht, D. (2002) *Shaping abortion discourse: Democracy and the public sphere in Germany and the United States*. Cambridge University Press, Cambridge.

Fox, J. R., Koloen, G., and Sahin, V. (2007) "No joke: A comparison of substance in *The Daily Show* with

Jon Stewart and broadcast network television coverage of the 2004 presidential election campaign," *Journal of Broadcasting & Electronic Media*, 51(2), pp. 213–27. doi: 10.1080/08838150701304621.

Fraser, N. (1992) "Rethinking the public sphere: A contribution to the critique of actually existing democracy." In: Calhoun, C. (ed.) *Habermas and the public sphere*. MIT Press, Cambridge, MA, pp. 109–42.

Fraser, N. (2009) "Theorie der Öffentlichkeit: Strukturwandel der Öffentlichkeit (1961)." In: Brunkhorst, H., Kreide, R., and Lafont, C. (eds.) *Habermas-Handbuch*. J. B. Metzler, Stuttgart, pp. 148–55.

Freelon, D. (2015) "Discourse architecture, ideology, and democratic norms in online political discussion," *New Media & Society*, 17(5), pp. 772–91. doi: 10.1177/146144481 3513259.

Fung, A. (2012) "Continuous institutional innovation and the pragmatic conception of democracy," *Polity*, 44(4), pp. 609–24. doi: 10.1057/pol.2012.17.

Garcez, R. L. O. and Maia, R. C. M. (2014) "The struggle for recognition of the deaf on the Internet: The political function of storytelling." In: Maia, R. C. M. *Recognition and the media*. Palgrave Macmillan, London, pp. 45–64.

Gastil, J. (2008) *Political communication and deliberation*. SAGE, Thousand Oaks, CA.

Gerhards, J., Neidhardt, F., and Rucht, D. (1998) *Zwischen Palaver und Diskurs: Strukturen öffentlicher Meinungsbildung am Beispiel der deutschen Diskussion zur Abtreibung*. Westdeutscher, Opladen.

Glover, R. W. (2012) "Games without frontiers? Democratic engagement, agonistic pluralism and the question of exclusion," *Philosophy & Social Criticism*, 38(1), pp. 81–104.

Golan, G. (2006) "Inter-media agenda setting and global news coverage: Assessing the influence of the

New York Times on three network television evening news programs," *Journalism Studies*, 7(2), pp. 323–33. doi: 10.1080/14616700500533643.

Göle, N. (2010) "Manifestations of the religious–secular divide: Self, state and the public sphere." In: Cady, L. E. and Shakman Hurd, E. (eds.) *Comparative secularisms in a global age*. Palgrave Macmillan, London, pp. 41–56.

Graham, T., Broersma, M., Hazelhoff, K., and van 't Haar, G. (2013) "Between broadcasting political messages and interacting with voters: The use of Twitter during the 2010 UK general election campaign," *Information, Communication & Society*, 16(5), pp. 692–716. doi: 10.1080/1369118X.2013.785581.

Gurevitch, M. and Blumler, J. G. (1990) "Political communication systems and democratic values." In: Lichtenberg, J. (ed.) *Democracy and the mass media*. Cambridge University Press, Cambridge, pp. 269–89.

Gutmann, A. and Thompson, D. (1996) *Democracy and disagreement*. Harvard University Press, Cambridge, MA.

Habermas, J. (1975) *Legitimation crisis*. Beacon Press, Boston, MA.

Habermas, J. (1984) *The theory of communicative action. Volume 1: Reason and the rationalization of society*. Beacon Press, Boston, MA.

Habermas, J. (1987a) *The philosophical discourse of modernity*. MIT Press, Cambridge, MA.

Habermas, J. (1987b) *The theory of communicative action. Volume 2: Lifeworld and system – A critique of functionalist reason*. Beacon Press, Boston, MA.

Habermas, J. (1989a) *The structural transformation of the public sphere*. Polity, Cambridge.

Habermas, J. (1989b) *Vorstudien und Ergänzungen zur Theorie des kommunikativen Handelns*. Suhrkamp, Frankfurt.

Habermas, J. (1990) "Discourse ethics: Notes on a program of philosophical justification." In: Habermas, J. *Moral consciousness and communicative action*. Polity, Cambridge, pp. 43–115.

Habermas, J. (1992) "Further reflections on the public sphere." In: Calhoun, C. (ed.) *Habermas and the public sphere*. MIT Press, Cambridge, MA, pp. 421–61.

Habermas, J. (1994) "Three normative models of democracy," *Constellations*, 1(1), pp. 1–10. doi: 10.1111/j.1467-8675.1994.tb00001.x.

Habermas, J. (1996) *Between facts and norms: Contributions to a discourse theory of law and democracy*. MIT Press, Cambridge, MA.

Habermas, J. (1998) "A genealogical analysis of the cognitive content of morality." In: Habermas, J. *The inclusion of the other: Studies in political theory*. MIT Press, Cambridge, MA, pp. 3–46.

Habermas, J. (2006a) "Political communication in media society: Does democracy still enjoy an epistemic dimension? The impact of normative theory on empirical research," *Communication Theory*, 16(4), pp. 411–26. doi: 10.1111/j.1468-2885.2006.00280.x

Habermas, J. (2006b) "Religion in the public sphere," *European Journal of Philosophy*, 14(1), pp. 1–25. doi: 10.1111/j.1468-0378.2006.00241.x.

Habermas, J. (2008) "Public space and political public sphere: The biographical roots of two motifs in my thought." In: Habermas, J. *Between naturalism and religion*. Polity, Cambridge, pp. 11–23.

Habermas, J. (2009a) "Media, markets and consumers: The quality press as the backbone of the political public sphere." In: Habermas, J. *Europe: The faltering project*. Polity, Cambridge, pp. 131–7.

Habermas, J. (2009b) "Political communication in media society: Does democracy still have an epistemic dimension?" In: Habermas, J. *Europe: The faltering project.* Polity, Cambridge, pp. 138–83.

Hall, S. (1980) "Encoding/Decoding." In: Hall, S., Hobson, D., Lowe, A., and Willis, P. (eds.) *Culture, media, language.* Hutchinson, London, pp. 166–76.

Hallin, D. C. and Mancini, P. (2004) *Comparing media systems: Three models of media and politics.* Cambridge University Press, Cambridge.

Hargittai, E., Gallo, J., and Kane, M. (2008) "Cross-ideological discussions among conservative and liberal bloggers," *Public Choice*, 134(1), pp. 67–86. doi: 10.1007/s11127-007-9201-x.

Hart, R. P. (2013) "The rhetoric of political comedy: A tragedy?" *International Journal of Communication*, 7, pp. 338–70.

Hart, R. P. and Hartelius, E. J. (2007) "The political sins of Jon Stewart," *Critical Studies in Media Communication*, 24(3), pp. 263–72. doi: 10.1080/07393180701520991.

Hepp, A. and Wessler, H. (2009) "Politische Diskurskulturen: Überlegungen zur empirischen Erklärung segmentierter europäischer Öffentlichkeit," *Medien & Kommunikationswissenschaft*, 57(2), pp. 174–97.

Himelboim, I., McCreery, S., and Smith, M. (2013) "Birds of a feather tweet together: Integrating network and content analyses to examine cross-ideology exposure on Twitter," *Journal of Computer-Mediated Communication*, 18(2), pp. 40–60. doi: 10.1111/jcc4.12001.

Hindman, M. S. (2010) *The myth of digital democracy.* Princeton University Press, Princeton, NJ.

Holbert, L. R. (2013) "Developing a normative approach to political satire: An empirical perspective," *International Journal of Communication*, 7, pp. 305–23.

Holbert, R. L., Hmielowski, J., Jain, P., Lather, J., and Morey, A. (2011) "Adding nuance to the study of political humor effects: Experimental research on Juvenalian satire versus

Horatian satire," *American Behavioral Scientist*, 55(3), pp. 187–211. doi: 10.1177/0002764210392156.

Honneth, A. and Joas, H. (eds.) (1991) *Communicative action: Essays on Jürgen Habermas's The Theory of Communicative Action*. MIT Press, Cambridge, MA.

Huspek, M. (2007a) "Habermas and oppositional public spheres: A stereoscopic analysis of black and white press practices," *Political Studies*, 55(4), pp. 821–43. doi: 10.1111/j.1467-9248.2007.00661.x.

Huspek, M. (2007b) "Normative potentials of rhetorical action within deliberative democracies," *Communication Theory*, 17(4), pp. 356–66. doi: 10.1111/j.1468-2885.2007.00302.x.

Hyun, K. (2012) "Americanization of web-based political communication? A comparative analysis of political blogospheres in the United States, the United Kingdom, and Germany," *Journalism & Mass Communication Quarterly*, 89(3), pp. 397–413. doi: 10.1177/1077699012447919

Jackson, S. J. and Foucault Welles, B. (2016) "#Ferguson is everywhere: Initiators in emerging counterpublic networks," *Information, Communication & Society*, 19(3), pp. 397–418. doi: 10.1080/1369118X.2015.1106571.

Jacobson, T. (2017) "Trending theory of the public sphere," *Annals of the International Communication Association*, 41(1), pp. 70–82. doi: 10.1080/23808985.2017.1288070.

Jarren, O. and Vogel, M. (2011) "'Leitmedien' als Qualitätsmedien: Theoretisches Konzept und Indikatoren." In: Blum, R., Bonfadelli, H., Imhof, K., and Jarren, O. (eds.) *Krise der Leuchttürme öffentlicher Kommunikation*. VS Verlag für Sozialwissenschaften, Wiesbaden, pp. 17–29. doi: 10.1007/978-3-531-93084-8_2.

Jungherr, A. (2014) "The logic of political coverage on Twitter: Temporal dynamics and content," *Journal of*

Communication, 64(2), pp. 239–59. doi: 10.1111/jcom. 12087.

Kanra, B. (2012) "Binary deliberation: The role of social learning in divided societies," *Journal of Public Deliberation*, 8(1), Article 1. Available at: http://www.publicdeliberation. net/jpd/vol8/iss1/art1

Karpf, D. (2017) "Digital politics after Trump," *Annals of the International Communication Association*, 41(2), pp. 198–207. doi: 10.1080/23808985.2017.1316675.

Kleinen-von Königslöw, K. and Keel, G. (2012) "Localizing *The Daily Show*: The *heute-show* in Germany." In: Baym, G. and Jones, J. (eds.) *Not necessarily the news? News parody and political satire across the globe*. Routledge, London, pp. 65–78.

Koop, R. and Jansen, H. J. (2009) "Political blogs and blogrolls in Canada: Forums for democratic deliberation?" *Social Science Computer Review*, 27(2), pp. 155–73. doi: 10.1177/0894439308326297.

Kuhlmann, C. (1999) *Die öffentliche Begründung politischen Handelns: Zur Argumentationsrationalität in der politischen Massenkommunikation*. Westdeutscher, Opladen.

Maia, R. C. M. (2012) *Deliberation, the media and political talk*. Hampton Press, New York, NY.

Mansbridge, J. J. (1983) *Beyond adversary democracy*. University of Chicago Press, Chicago, IL.

McGuigan, J. (2005) "The cultural public sphere," *European Journal of Cultural Studies*, 8(4), pp. 427–43. doi: 10.1177/1367549405057827.

Mendonça, R. F. and Ercan, S. A. (2015) "Deliberation and protest: Strange bedfellows? Revealing the deliberative potential of 2013 protests in Turkey and Brazil," *Policy Studies*, 36(3), pp. 267–82. doi: 10.1080/01442872.2015.1065970.

Min, S.-J. (2015) "Occupy Wall Street and deliberative decision-making: Translating theory to practice,"

Communication, Culture & Critique, 8(1), pp. 73–89. doi: 10.1111/cccr.12074.

Morrell, M. E. (2010) *Empathy and democracy: Feeling, thinking, and deliberation*. Pennsylvania State University Press, State College, PA.

Mouffe, C. (1999) "Deliberative democracy or agonistic pluralism?" *Social Research*, 66(3), pp. 745–58.

Mouffe, C. (2013) *Agonistics: Thinking the world politically*. Verso, London.

Müller-Doohm, S. (2016) *Habermas: A biography*. Polity, Cambridge.

Mutz, D. C. (2006) *Hearing the other side: Deliberative versus participatory democracy*. Cambridge University Press, Cambridge.

Mutz, D. C. (2015) *In-your-face politics: The consequences of uncivil media*. Princeton University Press, Princeton, NJ.

Neblo, M. A. (2003) "Impassioned democracy: The role of emotion in deliberative theory." Unpublished manuscript. Available at: https://polisci.osu.edu/sites/polisci.osu.edu/files/NebloImpassioned4Web_0.pdf

Negt, O. and Kluge, A. (1972) *Öffentlichkeit und Erfahrung: Zur Organisationsanalyse von bürgerlicher und proletarischer Öffentlichkeit*. 4th edn. Suhrkamp, Frankfurt.

Neidhardt, F. (1994) "Jenseits des Palavers: Funktionen politischer Öffentlichkeit." In: Wunden, W. (ed.) *Öffentlichkeit und Kommunikationskultur*. J. F. Steinkopf, Stuttgart, pp. 19–30.

Nir, L. (2012) "Cross-national differences in political discussion: Can political systems narrow deliberation gaps?" *Journal of Communication*, 62(3), pp. 553–70.

Öncü, S. and Abele, T. S. (2015) "#DELIBERATION: Eine Methodenentwicklung und – Anwendung zur Analyse von Debatten auf Twitter." Unpublished master's thesis. University of Mannheim, Mannheim.

Papacharissi, Z. (2004). "Democracy online: Civility, politeness, and the democratic potential of online political discussion groups," *New Media & Society*, 6(2), pp. 259–83. doi: 10.1177/1461444804041444.

Papacharissi, Z. (2015) *Affective publics: Sentiment, technology, and politics*. Oxford University Press, Oxford.

Parkinson, J. (2016) "On scholarly metaphors, or, what is deliberative about deliberative democracy?" Available at: https://ecpr.eu/Filestore/PaperProposal/90e7f4de-c707-447e-8a9a-7def01a57b73.pdf

Parkinson, J. and Mansbridge, J. (eds.) (2012) *Deliberative systems: Deliberative democracy at the large scale*. Cambridge University Press, Cambridge.

Peters, B. (1993) *Die Integration moderner Gesellschaften*. Suhrkamp, Frankfurt.

Peters, B. (2008a) "Contemporary journalism and its contribution to a discursive public sphere." In: Wessler, H. (ed.) *Public deliberation and public culture: The writings of Bernhard Peters, 1993–2005*. Palgrave Macmillan, London, pp. 134–59.

Peters, B. (2008b) "On public deliberation and public culture: Reflections on the public sphere." In: Wessler, H. (ed.) *Public deliberation and public culture: The writings of Bernhard Peters, 1993–2005*. Palgrave Macmillan, London, pp. 68–118.

Peters, B. (2008c) "Public discourse, identity and the problem of democratic legitimacy." In: Wessler, H. (ed.) *Public deliberation and public culture: The writings of Bernhard Peters, 1993–2005*. Palgrave Macmillan, London, pp. 213–54.

Peters, B. (2008d). "The functional capacity of contemporary public spheres." In: Wessler, H. (ed.) *Public deliberation and public culture: The writings of Bernhard Peters, 1993–2005*. Palgrave Macmillan, London, pp. 121–33.

Peters, B. (2008e) "The meaning of the public sphere." In: Wessler, H. (ed.) *Public deliberation and public culture: The writings of Bernhard Peters, 1993–2005.* Palgrave Macmillan, London, pp. 33–67.

Rinke, E. M. (2016) "Mediated deliberation." In: Mazzoleni, G. (ed.) *The international encyclopedia of political communication.* John Wiley & Sons, Hoboken, pp. 1–15. doi: 10.1002/9781118541555.wbiepc189.

Rinke, E. M. and Röder, M. (2011) "Media ecologies, communication culture, and temporal-spatial unfolding: Three components in a communication model of the Egyptian regime change," *International Journal of Communication*, 5, pp. 1273–85.

Sanders, L. M. (1997) "Against deliberation," *Political Theory*, 25(3), pp. 347–76.

Schuessler, J. (2015) "After protests, *Charlie Hebdo* members receive standing ovation at PEN Gala," *New York Times*, May 6, p. A20.

Scudder, M. (2016) "Beyond empathy: Strategies and ideals of democratic deliberation." *Polity*, 48(4), pp. 524–50. doi: 10.1057/s41279-016-0001-9.

Shaw, A. and Benkler, Y. (2012) "A tale of two blogospheres: Discursive practices on the left and right," *American Behavioral Scientist*, 56(4), pp. 459–87.

Shephard, M. (2014) *Twittish tweets? Twitter's ability to be deliberative?* APSA 2014 Annual Meeting Paper.

Shin, Y., Gupta, M., and Myers, S. (2011) "Prevalence and mitigation of forum spamming." In: *INFOCOM, 2011 Proceedings*, Institute of Electrical and Electronics Engineers, pp. 2309–17. doi: 10.1109/INFCOM.2011.59 35048.

Squires, C. R. (2002) "Rethinking the black public sphere: An alternative vocabulary for multiple public spheres," *Communication Theory*, 12(4), pp. 446–68.

Steiner, J., Jaramillo, M. C., Maia, R. C. M., and Mameli, S. (2017) *Deliberation across deeply divided societies: Transformative moments.* Cambridge University Press, Cambridge.

Stellar, J. E., Gordon, A. M., Piff, P. K., Cordaro, D., Anderson, C. L., Bai, Y., Maruskin, L. A., and Keltner, D. (2017) "Self-transcendent emotions and their social functions: Compassion, gratitude, and awe bind us to others through prosociality," *Emotion Review*, 9(3), pp. 1–8. doi: 10.1177/1754073916684557.

Strömbäck, J. (2005) "In search of a standard: Four models of democracy and their normative implications for journalism," *Journalism Studies*, 6(3), pp. 331–45. doi: 10.1080/14616700500131950.

Stromer-Galley, J. and Wichowski, A. (2011) "Political discussion online." In: Consalvo, M. and Ess, C. (eds.), *The handbook of Internet studies.* Blackwell, Oxford, pp. 168–87.

Sunstein, C. R. (2007) *Republic.com 2.0.* Princeton University Press, Princeton, NJ.

Töpfl, F. and Piwoni, E. (2015) "Public spheres in interaction: Comment sections of news websites as counterpublic spaces," *Journal of Communication*, 65(3), pp. 465–88. doi: 10.1111/jcom.12156.

Tumasjan, A., Sprenger, T. O., Sandner, P. G., and Welpe, I. M. (2011) "Election forecasts with Twitter: How 140 characters reflect the political landscape," *Social Science Computer Review*, 29(4), pp. 402–18. doi: 10.1177/0894439310386557.

Wahl-Jorgensen, K. (2001) "Letters to the editor as a forum for public deliberation: Modes of publicity and democratic debate," *Critical Studies in Media Communication*, 18(3), pp. 303–20. doi: 10.1080/07393180128085.

Wahl-Jorgensen, K. (2013) "Future directions for political communication scholarship: Considering emotion in mediated public participation." In: Valdivia, A. N. (ed.) *The international encyclopedia of media studies*. Wiley-Blackwell, Hoboken, NJ, pp. 455–77.

Warner, M. (1992) "The mass public and the mass subject." In: Calhoun, C. (ed.) *Habermas and the public sphere*. MIT Press, Cambridge, MA, pp. 377–401.

Warner, M. (2005) *Publics and counterpublics*. Zone Books, New York, NY.

Wessler, H. (1999) *Öffentlichkeit als Prozess: Deutungsstrukturen und Deutungswandel in der deutschen Drogenberichterstattung*. Westdeutscher, Opladen.

Wessler, H. (2008) "Investigating deliberativeness comparatively," *Political Communication*, 25(1), pp. 1–22. doi: 10.1080/10584600701807752.

Wessler, H., Peters, B., Brüggemann, M., Kleinen-von Königslöw, K., and Sifft, S. (2008) *Transnationalization of public spheres*. Palgrave Macmillan, Basingstoke.

Wessler, H. and Rinke, E. M. (2012) "Öffentlichkeit." In: Mau, S. and Schöneck, N. M. (eds.) *Handwörterbuch zur Gesellschaft Deutschlands*. VS Verlag für Sozialwissenschaften, Wiesbaden, pp. 637–50.

Wessler, H. and Rinke, E. M. (2014) "Deliberative performance of television news in three types of democracy: Insights from the United States, Germany, and Russia," *Journal of Communication*, 64(5), pp. 827–51.

Wessler, H., Rinke, E. M., and Löb, C. (2016) "Should we be Charlie? A deliberative take on religion and secularism in mediated public spheres," *Journal of Communication*, 66(2), pp. 314–27. doi: 10.1111/jcom.12213.

Woolley, S. C. and Guilbeault, D. (2017) *Computational propaganda in the United States of America: Manufacturing consensus online*. Project on Computational Propaganda, Oxford.

Wrobel, I. [Tucholsky, K.] (1919) "Was darf die Satire?" *Berliner Tageblatt*, January 27.

Wrobel, I. [Tucholsky, K.] (1931) "Der bewachte Kriegsschauplatz," *Die Weltbühne*, August 4, p. 191.

Young, I. M. (1996) "Communication and the other: Beyond deliberative democracy." In: Benhabib, S. (ed.) *Democracy and difference: Contesting the boundaries of the political.* Princeton University Press, Princeton, NJ.

Young, I. M. (2000) *Inclusion and democracy.* Oxford University Press, Oxford.

INDEX